Cayden - 381-5-12

AF248820

Chinese Painting: An Escape from the "Dusty" World

By the side of the hamlet I built a thatched pavilion.
Balanced and squared, it is lofty in conception.
The woods being deep, birds are happy;
the dust being distant, bamboos and pines are clean.
Streams and rocks invite lingering enjoyment,
lutes and books please my temperament.
How should I bid farewell to the world of the
*   ordinary and the familiar,*
and let my heart go its own way for the
*   gratification of my life?*

Wu Chen, *Poetic Feeling in a Thatched Pavilion*, 1347

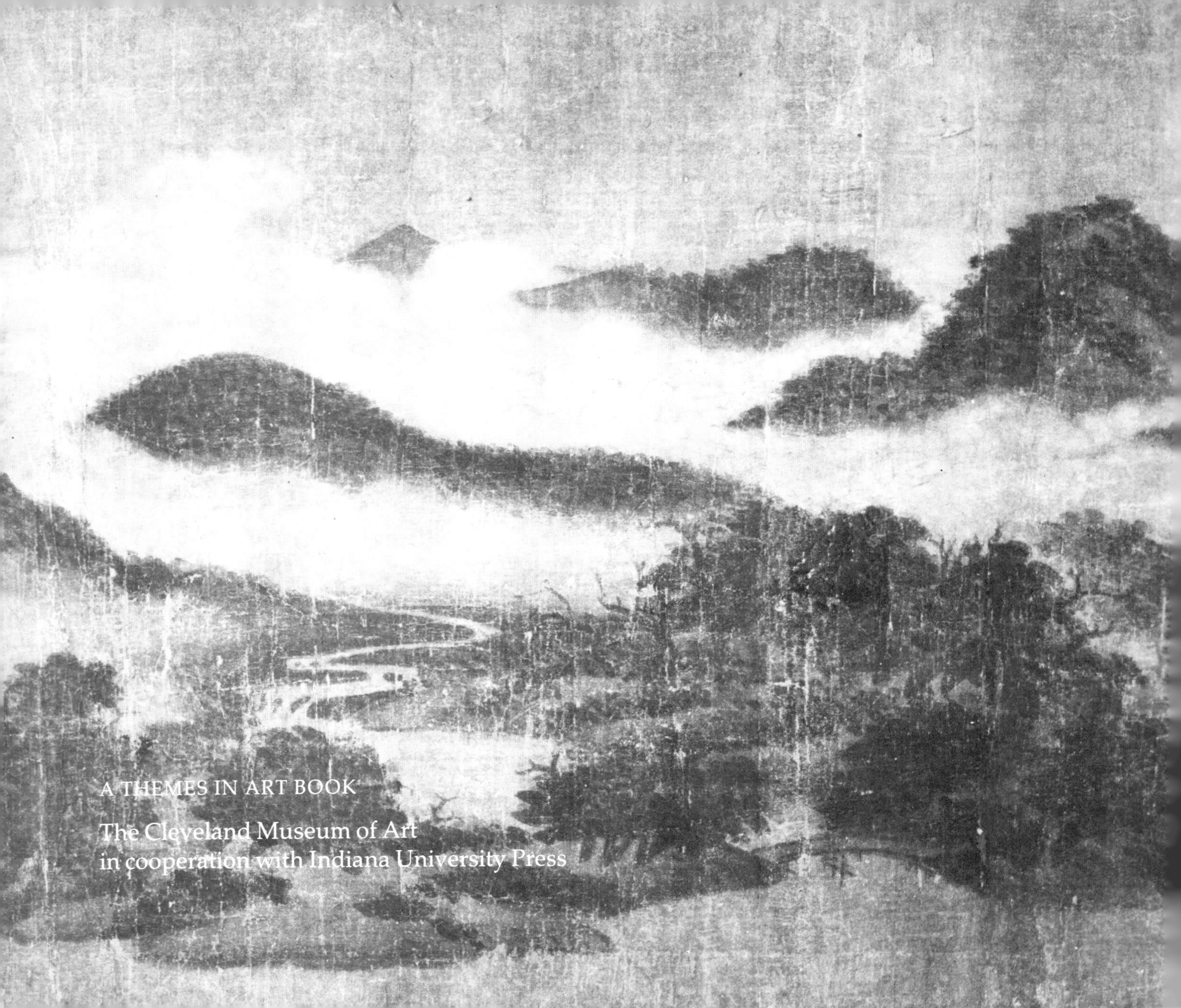
A THEMES IN ART BOOK

The Cleveland Museum of Art
in cooperation with Indiana University Press

Chinese Painting: An Escape from the "Dusty" World

MARJORIE L. WILLIAMS

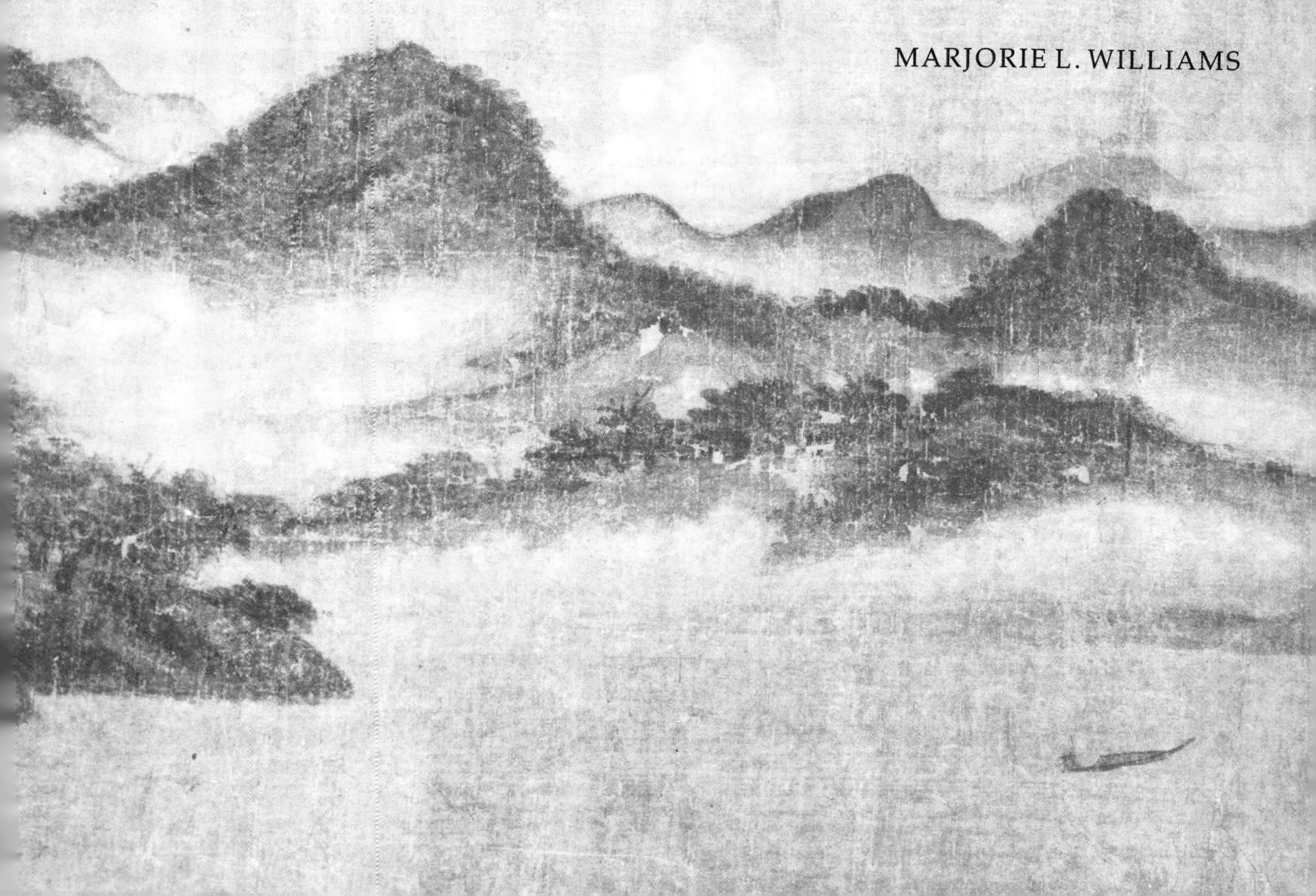

Published with the support of
the National Endowment for the Humanities

Distributed by Indiana University Press
Bloomington, Indiana 47405

LC 81-65665

Cover: Detail from the handscroll *Poetic Feeling in a Thatched Pavilion* by Wu Chen, Fig. 36

Contents

Chronology

Hsia Dynasty	twenty-first – sixteenth century BC
Shang Dynasty	sixteenth century – 1045 BC
Chou Dynasty	1045 – 256 BC
Spring and Autumn Period	722 – 481 BC
Warring States Period	480 – 221 BC
Ch'in Dynasty	221 – 206 BC
Han Dynasty	206 BC – AD 220
Six Dynasties	220 – 581
Sui Dynasty	581 – 618
T'ang Dynasty	618 – 906
Five Dynasties	906 – 960
Sung Dynasty	960 – 1279
Northern Sung	960 – 1127
Southern Sung	1127 – 1279
Yüan Dynasty	1279 – 1368
Ming Dynasty	1368 – 1644
Ch'ing Dynasty	1644 – 1911

Note

Bracketed numbers that follow caption illustrations are the numbers assigned to paintings in the exhibition catalog, and are included here for easy reference to *Eight Dynasties of Chinese Painting: The Collections of the Nelson Gallery-Atkins Museum, Kansas City, and The Cleveland Museum of Art*, with essays by Wai-kam Ho, Sherman E. Lee, Laurence Sickman, and Marc F. Wilson (Cleveland, Ohio: Cleveland Museum of Art, 1980).

Preface

The splendors of China's rich heritage have captivated Westerners, who are avidly establishing cultural and commercial exchanges with this land of over 800 million people. China's influence on the Western world is evident in the increased number of travelers lured, in part, to its borders by the prodigious archaeological discoveries of the past decade. For those unable to visit China, their curiosity can be partially satisfied in major department stores where fashions and household commodities reflect distinctive Chinese flavors.

Although contemporary China is subject to modern methods of investigation, most of traditional China—its history, philosophies, and arts—continues to hold many mysteries for the majority of Westerners. Bronzes, sculptures, and jades, dating from antiquity, are, of all China's arts, the most prevalent in the minds of museum visitors, especially those who saw the two archaeological exhibitions from China: The Exhibition of Archaeological Finds of the People's Republic of China (1974) and The Great Bronze Age of China (1980). Painting, a two-thousand-year-old artistic tradition, however, still seems "foreign" to many people even though European and American museums house masterpieces of Chinese painting. This unfamiliarity will undoubtedly disappear as these museums make their collections available through such exhibitions as Eight Dynasties of Chinese Painting: The Collections of the Nelson Gallery-Atkins Museum, Kansas City, and The Cleveland Museum of Art.

Certain principles, shared by the majority of Chinese painters regardless of their artistic classification, endured throughout the entire history of Chinese painting. The educational guide *Chinese Painting: An Escape from the "Dusty" World,* prepared in conjunction with the Eight Dynasties exhibition, introduces essential concepts that are rooted in ancient philosophies as well as an explanation of artists' tools, formats, themes, and techniques.

As a basic precept of Confucianism, a philosophy originating in the Chou Dynasty (1045–221 BC), veneration of antiquity is an innate tradition of Chinese painting. Chinese artists consistently referred to the paintings of older, accomplished artists and reverently adopted these past styles in their own works. Beyond this, however, Confucianism and the other indigenous Chinese philosophy, Taoism, fostered a love for nature's rational order and its spiritual aura. Artists studied its manifestations in the physical forms of rocks, trees, and mountains. This philosophical background nourished the lengthy development of landscape painting, the predominant theme of Chinese painting. All artists, whether striving to portray nature's models in a realistic, descriptive manner or to convey their personal emotions and virtuous characters, deferentially honored nature's majesties and the venerable masters of Chinese painting.

The text presented here complements the largely photographic educational exhibition, Chinese Painting:

Themes and Techniques. All the paintings illustrated in both the exhibition and guide are from the collections of The Nelson Gallery-Atkins Museum and The Cleveland Museum of Art. Accessories of the artist's studio were generously loaned to the Museum by Mr. and Mrs. Severance A. Millikin, Mr. and Mrs. Wai-kam Ho, and Mr. and Mrs. Marc F. Wilson.

The enjoyment in preparing this educational exhibition and accompanying guide was consulting, on a day-to-day basis, with the knowledgeable and enthusiastic staff of the Oriental Art Department. The old lament echoed by most education departments that curatorial personnel are uncooperative and non-communicative simply does not apply to this coterie. As Director of the Cleveland Museum and Chief Curator of the Oriental Department, Dr. Sherman E. Lee — both personally and through his numerous publications that are now standard texts — continues to inspire an appreciation for Chinese painting within and without the Museum. Wai-kam Ho, Curator of Chinese Art, imparted unrecorded knowledge with thoroughness and thoughtfulness, even when asked the most elemental questions concerning the scholar's studio and inkstones. Jean Cassill's cheerful efficiency speeded the acquisition of photographs and "misplaced" information. Elinor Pearlstein's unique wit and China-sense lightened the effort. Initially outlining the map, she also assisted Andrew T. Chakalis of the Extensions Division in its final preparation. Nora Liu's contagious spirit and advice as a contemporary Chinese artist revitalized art historical jargon. Joseph L. Finizia, designer of the exhibition, created a coherent, innovative setting that enhanced the exhibition as a visual and an educational experience.

Among those who worked directly with the manuscript, I am indebted to Joy Walworth, a discriminating editor whose curiosity and sensitivity to the intricacies of the language was a sustaining motivation throughout all stages of the publication. I am particularly grateful that Amy Levine typed the manuscript. *Chinese Painting: An Escape from the "Dusty" World* is a part of the Themes in Art series published under the general editorship of Dr. Gabriel P. Weisberg, Curator of the Department of Art History and Education. My heartfelt thanks to all.

The publication was funded by the National Endowment for the Humanities.

A Linear Art

Chinese painting is one of the greatest of all the world's arts, yet contemporary Westerners living over a thousand years after Chang Yen-yüan echo his observation that Chinese paintings are "strange" or unfamiliar in both appearance and themes. Indeed, Chinese paintings do look entirely different when compared with those European and American works that were painted on wooden panels or framed canvases. They differ in format, artistic materials, and techniques.

All Eastern artists traditionally worked on flexible, or "portable," formats that included hanging scrolls (see Figs. 14, 18), handscrolls (see Foldout Fig. 4, Fig. 36), and album leaves (see Figs. 1, 12). Vertical hanging scrolls were more commonly used by Chinese artists before the twelfth century, at which time horizontal handscrolls and album leaves became popular. Hanging scrolls and handscrolls were kept rolled up until they were viewed. Album leaves were frequently combined to form a volume or book.

Silk, paper, brush, and ink are the relatively simple, yet extremely varied materials of the Chinese artist. Silk fabric, used as a painting ground as early as the third century BC, was woven especially for painting and differed from the cloth used in dressmaking. Each historic era is characterized by the type of silk it manufactured. T'ang Dynasty (618–906) fabric was thick and coarse, while Sung Dynasty (960–1279) cloth ranged in texture from an extraordinarily fine, tight weave to a thicker, coarser weave. To make the fabric less absorbent and create a smooth surface, Chinese painters sized the cloth with a solution of alum and glue. The silk grounds of Chinese paintings, now darkened with age, were originally a creamy white to light beige color.

After the thirteenth century, paper largely replaced silk as the preferred painting medium. Although Westerners may immediately think of rice paper as a product common among Eastern countries, it is coarse and unsuitable for painting. The varieties of paper used for painting were made from hemp fiber, bamboo, cotton, the bark of mulberry trees, and cocoons of silkworms. During the Ming Dynasty (1368–1644) the number of different papers increased, some even being imported from such neighboring countries as Korea. The individual artist selected the variety of paper most suitable to his brushwork. Absorbent papers were used for rich, wet brushstrokes (see Fig. 11), while those made hard by sizing with an alum-and-glue solution were chosen to achieve drier brush techniques (see Fig. 29).

Black, water-base ink (see Fig. 43) and bamboo-handled brushes (see Fig. 47) with animal-hair tips were the vehicles of artistic expression used by both Chinese writers and artists. They prepared the liquid ink by grinding the solid ink stick, or cake, on a polished, finely textured stone (see Fig. 40). Created from pine soot (or carbon) and gum (or glue), molded ink cakes were often elaborately decorated. Pine-soot ink, derived from the burnt core of the pine tree, first appeared during the Han Dynasty (206 BC–AD 220).

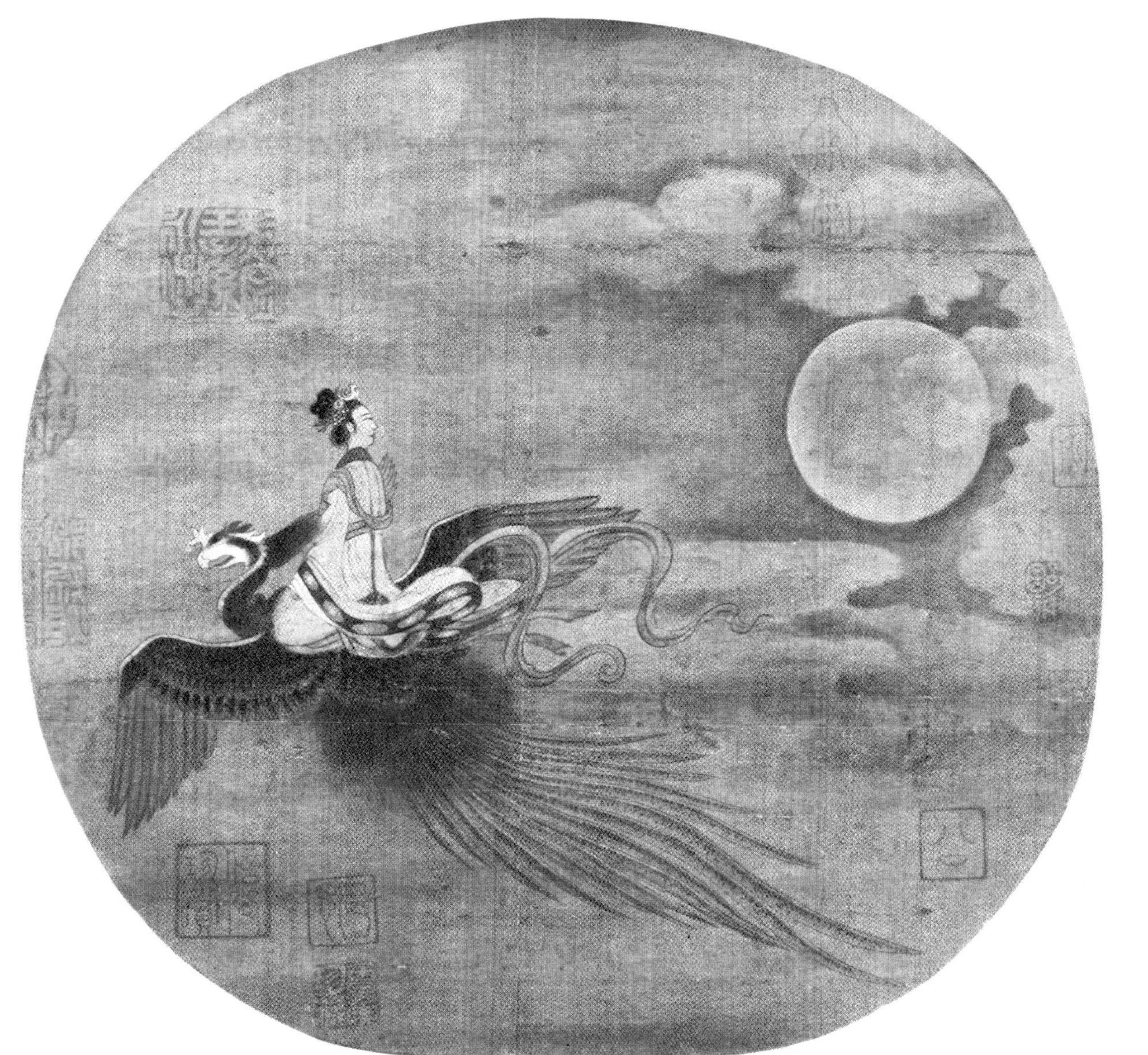

Chang Yu (active 1064–1085), an imperial ink maker working during the eleventh century, improved the pine-soot ink so that it looked shiny and black on the painted surface by combining pine soot, oil soot, deer gum, and an unnecessary but delightful ingredient —perfume.

The artist was the master and his brush the servant. Although a few of China's eccentric artists painted with their fingers, nails, toes, and hair, the majority of painters used a brush to apply ink onto the silk or paper ground. The most important part of this artistic instrument is the bristled end, made of soft rabbit's and wolf's fur or stiffer pony's hair or mouse's whiskers. The stiffness or softness of the brush was not only dependent upon the type of hair but also whether or not it was treated with glue. An untreated, soft brush lost its point when soaked in ink and water and had to be reshaped. Stiff brushes, treated with glue, retained their tips even after use. Artists carefully chose the correct brush for their painting styles. To create an even, linear brushstroke, Chang Wu selected a soft brush for his illustration of *The Nine Songs* (Fig. 3), while Yen Hui (Figs. 4, 5) used stiff brushes to attain fluctuating and uneven lines.

Ironically, although Chinese paintings are distinguished from Western paintings in many respects, Eastern and Western artists shared a basic instructional technique: they learned to paint by studying and copying the works of older, established artists. This training method, an artistic convention common to all Chinese artists, also reflected an innate respect for antiquity.

Veneration of the past was the founding principle of Confucianism, the indigenous philosophy permeating every facet of Chinese society.

Dominating traditional China from the first century BC through the early twentieth century, Confucianism promulgated an ordered and ethical society. The teachings of the sage-philosopher Confucius remained such a predominant force that the other major religions, Buddhism and Taoism, never replaced the older philosophy. Confucius believed in the existence of a moral order in nature and maintained that man could acquire perfect virtue through the study of former models of excellence. He heralded past peaceful epochs such as the founding years of the Chou Dynasty as moral societies and designated the legendary kings, Shao and Yun, as paragons of wisdom and virtue. Confucius viewed himself as a "transmitter, not a creator" and proudly proclaimed his dedication to the past: "I believe in and have a passion for the ancients."[1]

Chinese artists were, however, both transmitters and creators. Hsieh Ho, an early sixth-century artist and writer, established in his work *Old Record of the Classification of Painters* (*Ku Hua P'in Lu*) six principles for determining a "good" painting. The sixth condition, "transmission [of the experiences of the past] in making copies,"[2] reiterates Confucius' respect for historic models. Chinese painters learned from the works of older artists and added to this accumulative knowledge their own creative talents. As a method of study that aided in formulating a personal style, copying thus paid tribute to the ancient masters of Chinese painting.

A Goddess Carried Away on a Phoenix (Fig. 1), a small album painting by an anonymous eighteenth-century artist, is a copy of an earlier, twelfth-century work (Fig. 2) now in the collection of the Palace Museum, Peking, China. Both paintings exemplify the traditional study

Fig. 1. *A Goddess Carried Away on a Phoenix.* Album leaf, ink and color on silk. Artist unknown, Ch'ing Dynasty, 18th century. Anonymous loan.

techniques of Chinese painters. The later artist copied a six-hundred-year-old representation of a beautiful goddess carried into the heavens on the back of a phoenix. Obvious alterations and additions by the eighteenth-century artist indicate his painting is not an exact reproduction. He omitted the shadowy shapes in the moon and flattened the surrounding clouds to colored patterns. He further enhanced the seated figure by adding decorative motifs to the trailing scarves.

In copying the older painting, this anonymous artist faithfully selected the oval, fan-shaped format that by the eighteenth century was no longer fashionable. Stiff fan paintings that could be attached to a single wooden shaft were popular during the twelfth century. The folding fan (see Fig. 28), introduced to China from Japan during the Ming Dynasty, later became the more stylish painting format and provided the artist with two sides on which to both paint and write. These formats — the older round fan and the later "accordion" fan — were generally made into album leaves to provide for easier viewing and preservation as works of art.

Chinese painting is basically a linear art. The album paintings (Figs. 1, 2) demonstrate the creative process: both artists initially outlined their figures with black brushstrokes and filled in the boundaries with subtle colors. Such outlining strokes are called the "bones" of a painting and reveal the very structure of its composition. In contrast, paintings such as the twelfth-century handscroll *Cloudy Mountains* (see Fig. 11) by Mi Yu-jen, primarily devoid of linear structure, are classified as "boneless" creations. Mi Yu-jen built up the soft, rounded mountain forms using a "dotting" technique, juxtaposing and overlapping his brushstrokes. Once an outlining stroke defines the painted form, the linear quality will always remain evident even when mineral or vegetable colors and ink washes that range

in tonality from dark, rich black to pale, watery gray are added to the outline.

The outlining stroke can serve either as a boundary line simply defining shapes or as a descriptive, expressive line creating the illusion of a three-dimensional form. These differing characteristics of the black-ink brush line are determined by the type of brush the artist uses and how he manipulates that creative tool. Early in the history of Chinese painting these diverse brush techniques became two differentiated linear styles. The works of the later fourteenth-century artists Chang Wu (Fig. 3) and Yen Hui (Foldout Fig. 4, and Fig. 5) illustrate these two linear traditions of Chinese painting. Like all Chinese artists, the painters consciously chose those techniques that would enhance their theme.

Chang Wu, a master with absolute control of his artistic materials, painted four handscrolls illustrating *The Nine Songs* (Fig. 3). This collection of ritualistic hymns was written in the third century BC by Ch'ü Yüan after his banishment to the southern state of Ch'u. Based upon rural, sacred hymns of this region, his songs are invocations to the gods. In illustrating the fifth song, Chang depicted the Lord of Fate as a scholar dressed in his customary robes and carrying a staff and handscroll. He and his female attendant stand on patterned, curling clouds. His long robes gently billow in the air to convey the impression of a spirit-like weightlessness, and are defined with a sharp, elegant line unvarying in width. Chang initially outlined the mythical figures with a light gray ink and then painted over his underpainting with darker ink. Because there is little allow-

Fig. 2. *A Goddess Carried Away on a Phoenix.* Album leaf, ink and color on silk. Artist unknown, Sung Dynasty, 12th century. Palace Museum, Peking, China.

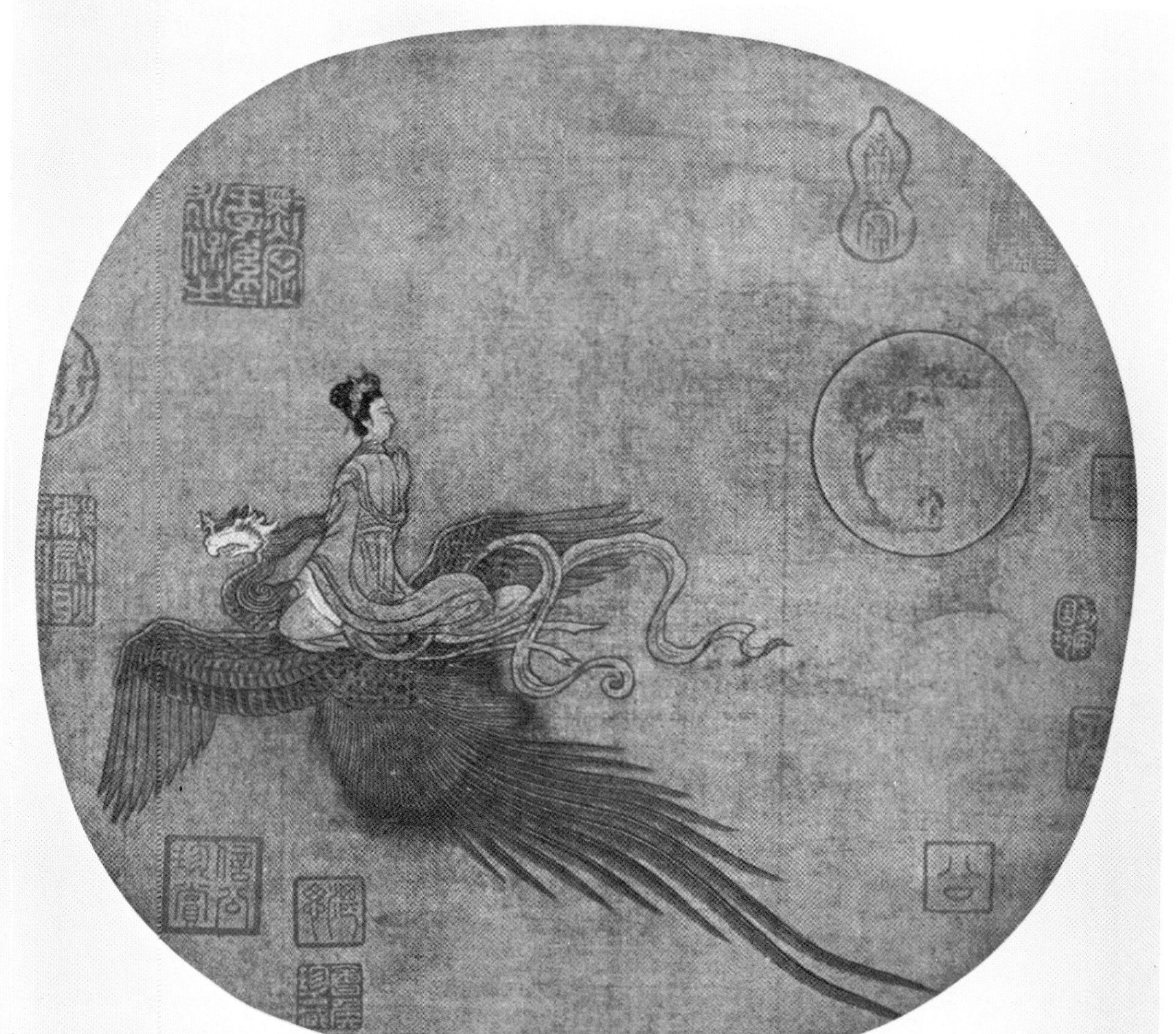

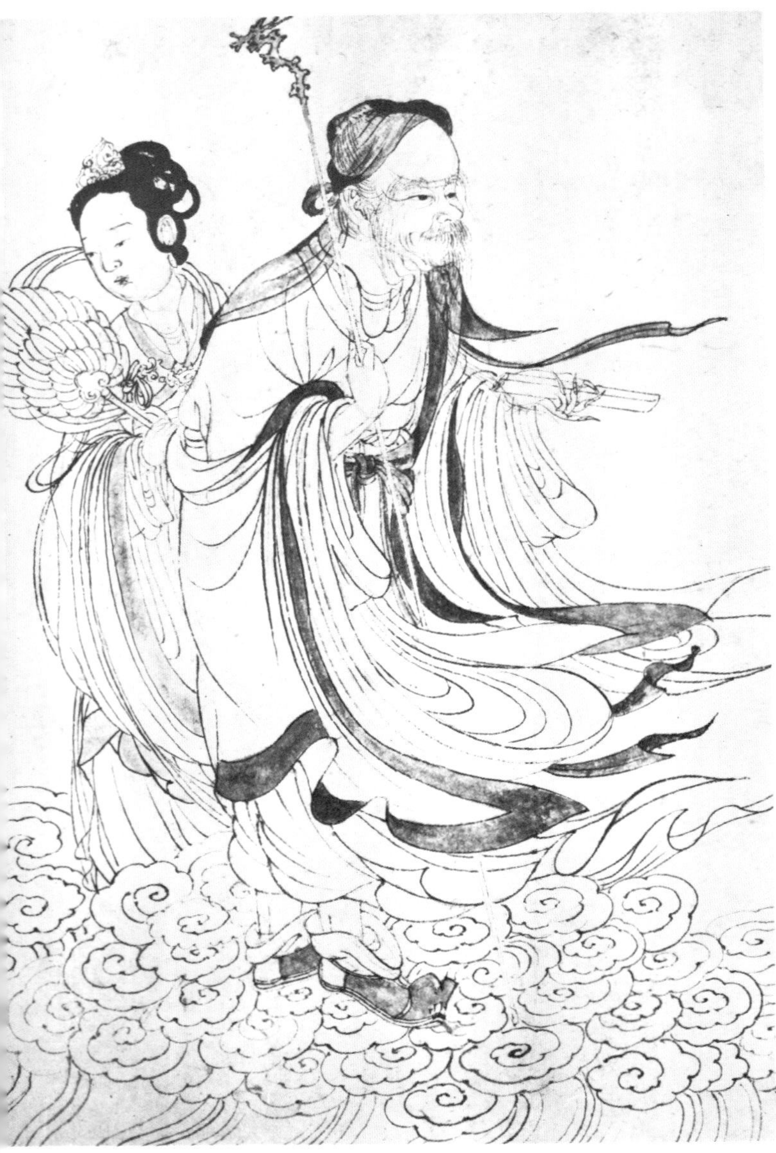

Fig. 3. *The Nine Songs* (detail). Handscroll, ink on paper, dated 1361. Chang Wu, active 1335–1365, Yüan Dynasty. Purchase from the J. H. Wade Fund. CMA 59.138 [96]

ance for revision when painting with water-base ink, this underpainting or "sketching" method was often used by artists working in the fine-line style.

Similar to nature's perfect creation — silk thread — the linear brushstroke is called the "spring-silkworm-spinning-thread" stroke. The elegant style of painting epitomizes the classical *pai-miao* (ink outline drawing without color) tradition that originated as early as the fourth century and can be traced through succeeding artistic generations. It is most often associated with the twelfth-century artist Li Kung-lin (1049–1106) who first illustrated "The Nine Songs," and whose now lost works were the prototype for Chang Wu's handscroll. Already a thousand-year-old painting tradition by the time Chang completed his scroll, the highly controlled, formal brushwork appropriately conveys the celestial stateliness of the fateful deity.

Another handscroll, *The Lantern Night Excursion of Chung K'uei* (Foldout Fig. 4) by Yen Hui, illustrates a legendary theme and a style of painting developed during the late T'ang Dynasty. Chung K'uei, a seventh-century contestant in the advanced civil service examination that determined those men eligible for governmental offices, is the focus of the painting. The frustrated scholar, who had studied most of his life in order to achieve this goal, killed himself after failing to pass the examina-tion. Legends recount that Chung K'uei, wearing the clothes of a scholar, appeared in the dream of Emperor Ming-huang as a large victorious demon wresting from another demon the purple bag and jade flute belonging to the emperor's consort Yang

Kuei-fei. The grateful emperor honored him with a
court burial. In return, Chung K'uei became a queller of
demons.

Yen Hui depicts Chung K'uei on a nocturnal excursion accompanied by a bizarre entourage of musicians, acrobats, and warriors. Like most of China's handscrolls, this painting should be viewed by beginning at the right side and progressing toward the left end of the scroll. Handscrolls were intended to be unrolled a few feet at a time so that the painting's images slowly emerged, revealing sudden unexpected surprises that enhanced the viewing pleasure. For this reason the handscroll format is often compared to a musical composition that flows from one progression into another, changing from loud to soft or from fast to slow. Yen Hui's handscroll begins with the leader beating a gong to announce a parade of muscular "show-offs." Devoid of background landscape to "set the stage," the viewer concentrates solely upon the humorous creatures who demonstrate their prowess; they lift rocks, stand on their hands, balance a pot. At this point, if actually unrolling the painting, the tempo quickens and the unsuspecting viewer is confronted with armed warriors swaggering across the silk, intimidating through military bravado. The furor passes and calmer servants transport chairs, a Chinese lute, or *ch'in*, and paintings bundled into a backpack. Others offer refreshment to the scholarly hero. Chung K'uei, shown riding on the shoulders of his attendants, brings up the rear of the parade and concludes the scroll.

In contrast to Chang Wu's fine outlining brushstroke, Yen Hui manipulates his brush so the width of the line varies, becoming thick, then thin (Fig. 5). This outlining stroke not only defines Chung K'uei's robes but also in-

Fig. 5. *The Lantern Night Excursion of Chung K'uei* (detail).

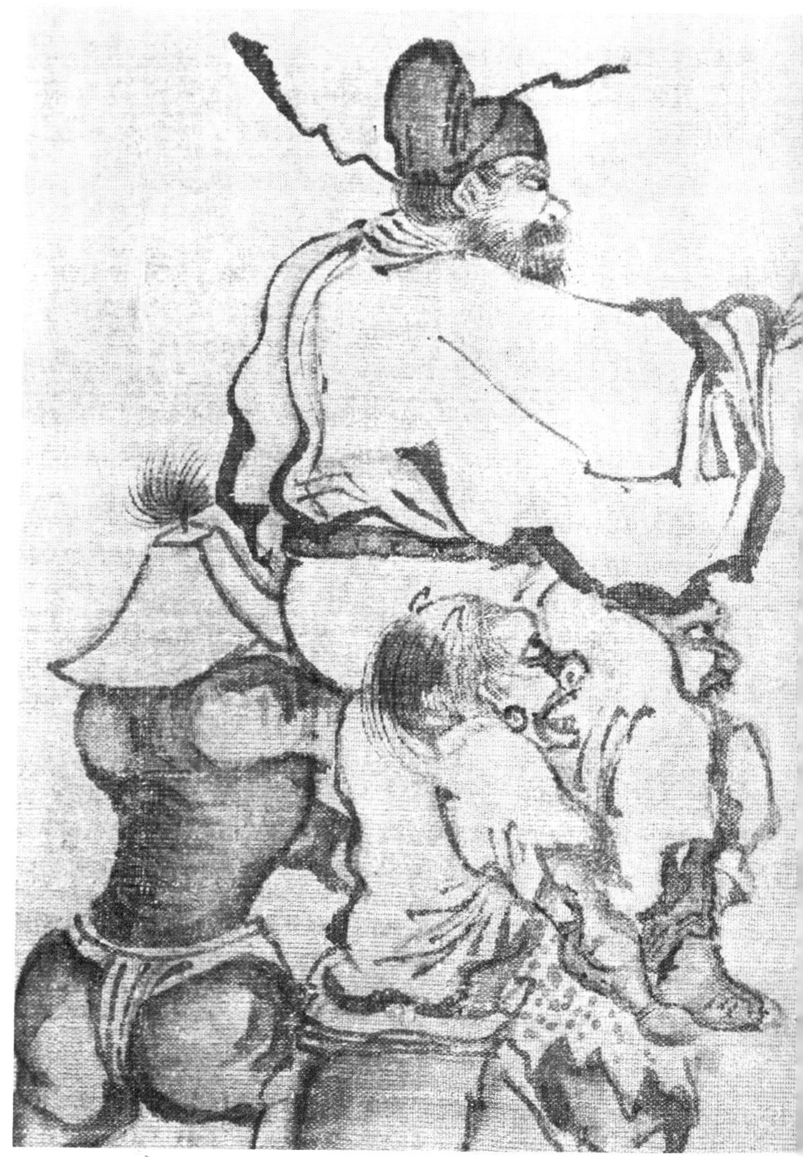

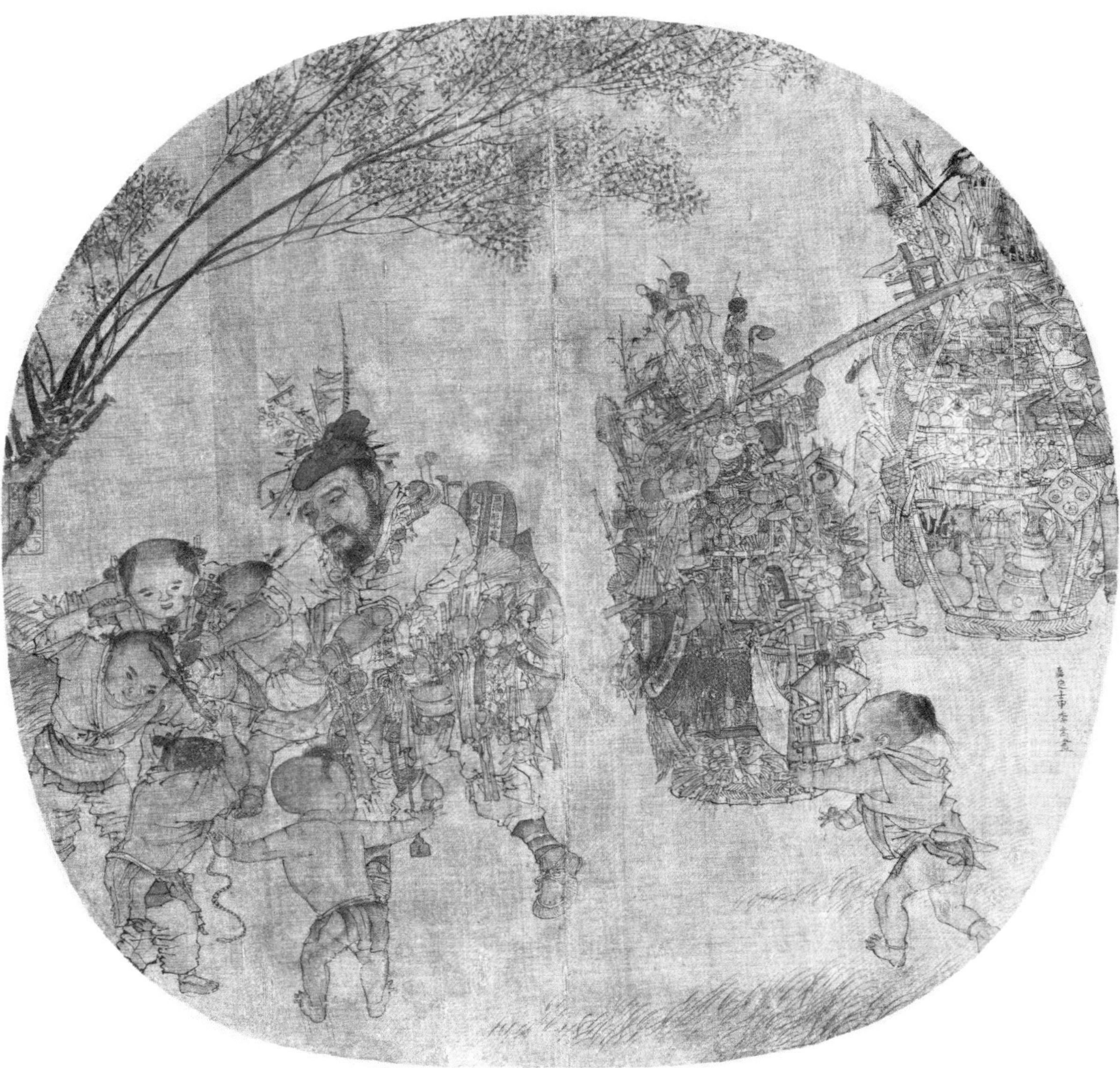

dicates the volume or bulkiness of his cloak. The energetic painter Wu Tao-tzu (active 720–760), famous for his paintings of demons, originated this descriptive brush style. While inappropriate for Chang Wu's formal paintings of the heavenly diety, Yen Hui's style successfully conveys the energy and earthy nature of a demon-stalker.

Yen Hui combined this indigenous Chinese linear style with the foreign painting technique of modeling three-dimensional forms in light and shade. Originating in Central Asia, the technique associated with the "demon" theme entered China during the T'ang Dynasty. Yen Hui's skillful use of illusionistic shading emphasizes the exaggerated musculature of the humorous, demonic figures.

Chang Wu's and Yen Hui's handscrolls are included in the category of figure painting — one of the major thematic classifications of Chinese painting. Appearing as early as the third century BC, figure painting continued as a dominant theme of Chinese painting until the middle of the eleventh century. At that time, landscape largely superseded figure painting, which lost its original dominance.

Figure painting flourished under the patronage of Confucianism, Buddhism, Taoism, and the imperial court.[3] Exemplary and didactic in purpose, the earliest figural compositions illustrated Confucian paragons. With the introduction of Buddhism, hieratic compositions of sacred dieties and other religious themes increased the number of figural themes. Secular themes, including women of the court or children at play, appealed to those Chinese emperors who surrounded themselves with artisans and established painting academies at their courts.

The T'ang Dynasty, the classical era of figure painting, and the succeeding Sung Dynasty (960–1279) are historic eras when figure painting developed under strong imperial support. The majority of linear styles used in figural compositions were based on the familiar *pai-miao* tradition (Fig. 3) and Wu Tao-tzu's energetic style (Fig. 5). Artists working in the Southern Sung Painting Academy during the twelfth and thirteenth centuries developed variations on these linear techniques.

The Knickknack Peddler (Fig. 6) reveals a favorite theme during this era that challenged artists to demonstrate their skills as draftsmen. Completed in 1212 and about nine inches high, this small fan painting is one of only three dated paintings by the artist Li Sung (active 1190–1230) sharing the theme of peddlers and urchins. Trained as a carpenter while he was young, the fastidious Li Sung served in the Southern Sung Painting Academy under three emperors. His work demonstrates the type of genre themes and nervous brush techniques popular among his contemporaries.

Abandoning his brimming baskets, the peddler with mallet raised rushes to aid a circle of animated children pelting a snake with rocks and sticks. Not wishing to miss the excitement, one young boy races with outstretched hands toward the intent group while a more timid child observes the commotion from the safety of the peddler's laden baskets.

Li Sung's brushwork is precise, nervous, and descriptive (Fig. 7). Fine, even lines define the profusion of gadgets bulging from his baskets, while quick, angular strokes successfully indicate the youngsters' rumpled trousers and jackets. The "nail-head" stroke, so named

Fig. 6. *The Knickknack Peddler.* Album leaf, ink and color on silk, dated 1212. Li Sung, active 1190–1230, Southern Sung Dynasty. Purchase, Andrew R. and Martha Holden Jennings Fund. CMA 63.582 [35]

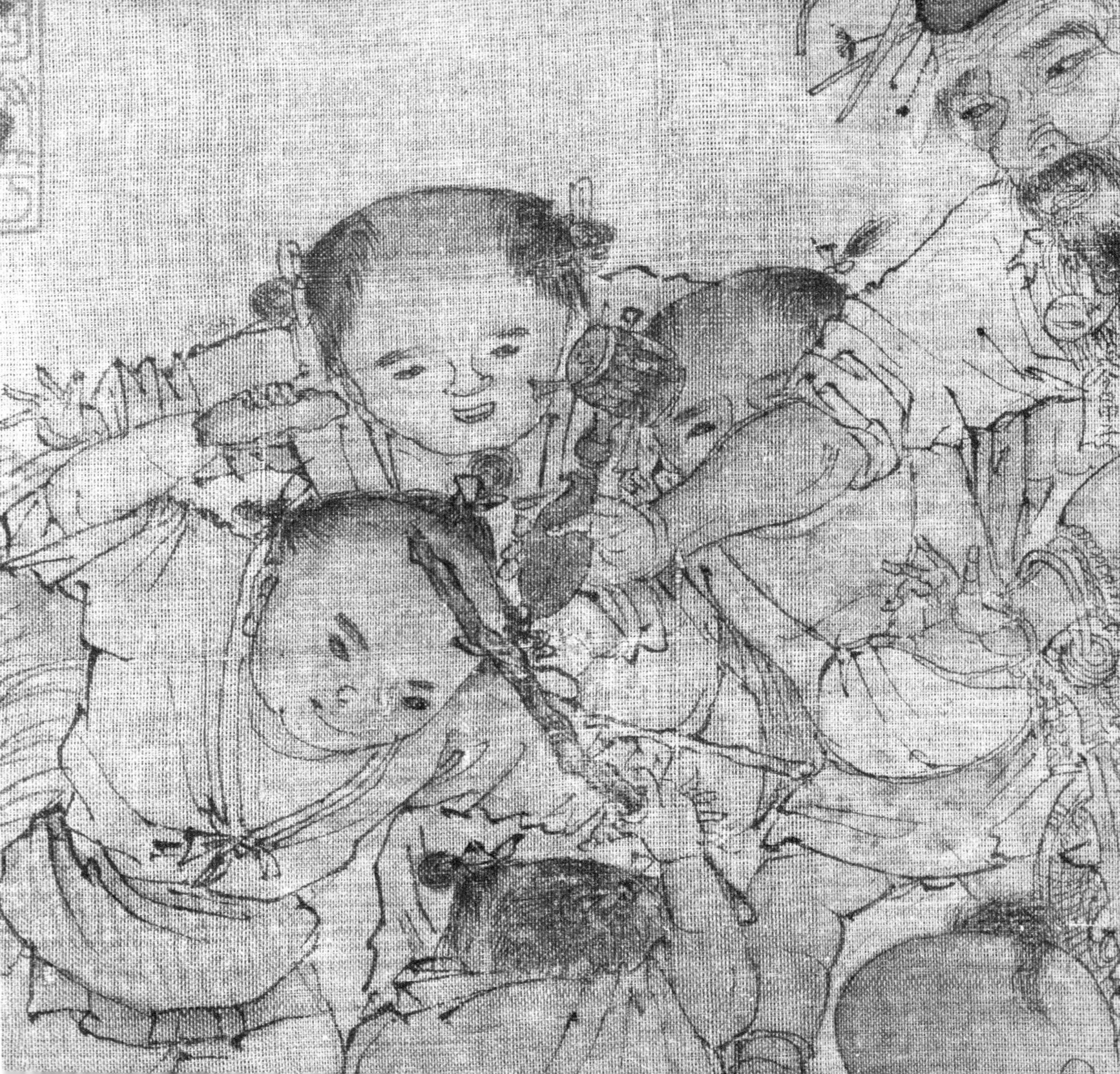

because of its thick "head" and made by applying pressure to the tip of the brush at the beginning of a stroke that then tapers to a point, is easily discernable in the folds of the disheveled clothing.

Li Sung's technical skills convincingly describe his subjects and are matched only by his ability to capture the psychological nuances of age and expression. Tightly knit into a circular composition, the children's round, youthful faces with intense, excited expressions are contrasted with the peddler's older, weathered face creased with astonishment and concern.

Chang Wu and Yen Hui lived during the fourteenth century of the Yüan Dynasty (1279–1368). This era marked a historic schism in Chinese painting. Artists working prior to this date professed and pursued different aesthetic criteria from those artists living after this short period lasting only eighty-nine years. During the centuries between the Han and Sung dynasties, artists strove to faithfully re-create nature's models through painted images. Li Sung's small masterpiece reflects the aesthetic attitudes prevalent during the Sung Dynasty, the pinnacle of realism in Chinese painting. Themes — whether of landscapes, figures, birds, flowers, or insects — were considered the only true reason for painting. Techniques played a subordinate, supporting role. The classical centuries of Chinese painting are distinguished by the great tenth- and eleventh-century landscape artists, China's old masters Li Ch'eng (see Fig. 14) and Chü-jan (see Fig. 18), as well as court painters like Ma Yüan (see Fig. 22), who were members of the imperial painting academies. All followed the same canonical fidelity to nature.

The literati, or scholars, who were also painters, and those professional artists patronized by the wealthy landowners and merchants during the fifteenth and sixteenth centuries became innovative forces during the following epoch of Chinese painting. The late thirteenth century witnessed a complete upheaval in Chinese society. Invading Mongols, following the early inroads of the great Genghis Khan, conquered China and abolished age-old institutions and customs. The most significant of these for the art of painting was the Painting Academy. Without strong, imperial patronage, the court academicians faded into anonymity and the literati quickly assumed an assertive position, becoming the avant-garde of the fourteenth century. Literati painters discarded earlier aesthetic guidelines. Although thematic content remained important, it narrowed to a few acceptable categories, including landscape and the "Three Friends" — pine, bamboo, plum blossom. Individualistic and expressive brush techniques accompanied these themes, and painted forms thus were thought to reveal the artist's personality and character rather than nature's reality. Although literati masters such as Chao Meng-fu (see Fig. 29), Wu Chen (see Fig. 36 and Cover), and Ni Tsan (see Fig. 37) recall classical artistic styles before the fourteenth century, their paintings display distinctive differences. Literati canons directed the last traditional centuries of Chinese painting. Old masters, court academicians, literati, and professional painters all contributed diverse styles, themes, and techniques to create the tradition of Chinese painting, a linear art that endured for two thousand years.

Fig. 7. *The Knickknack Peddler* (detail).

The opening quotation is taken from Osvald Siren, *The Chinese on the Art of Painting* (New York: Schocken Books, 1963), pp. 227–28.

Landscape, Nature, and Old Masters

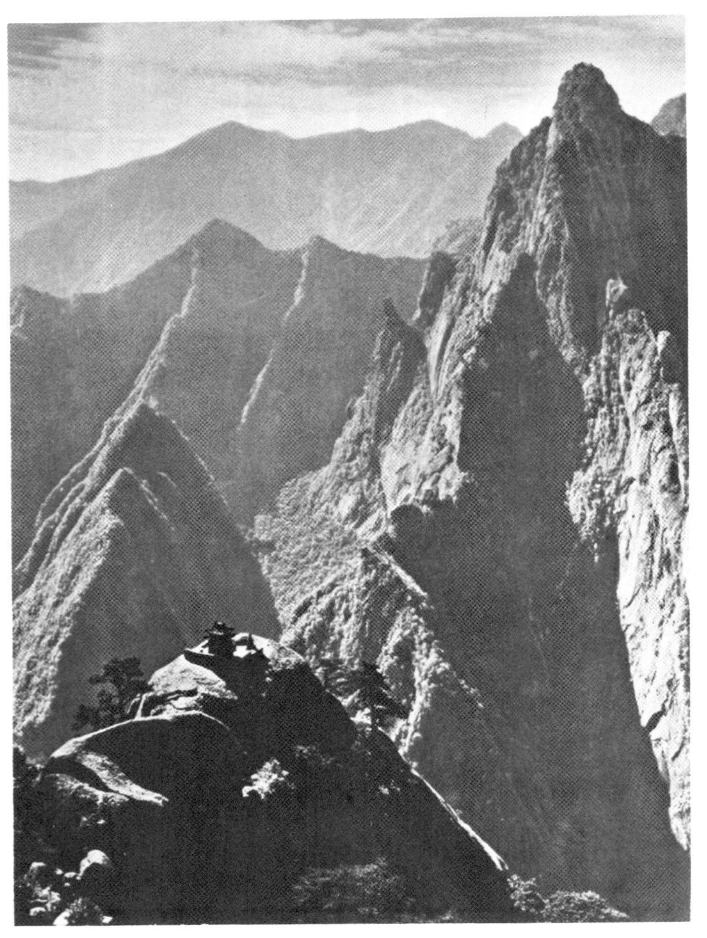

Westerners unfamiliar with China's geography are startled to discover that the towering peaks and mist-veiled mountains — repeated themes of Chinese landscape painters — actually do resemble the native Chinese countryside. People living in a nation distinguished by such dramatic contrasts in landscape as the western Colorado peaks and the southern Mississippi bayous never consider that China, as a land of over three million square miles, also harbors diverse terrains. Chinese landscape paintings are not fictional creations of artistic imaginations. Embodying stylistic conventions of the old masters, these paintings of "mountains and water" (*shan-shui*) eulogize the beauties of China's natural topography.

Located in the northwestern province of Shenhsi, Hua shan (Fig. 8) is one of the five sacred mountains symbolic of the five directions (north, south, east, west, center). Its seemingly uninhabitable, barren cliffs characterize the rugged terrain common to northern China. Entitled *Verdant Mountains* (Fig. 9), the handscroll by the twelfth-century artist Chiang Shen is Hua shan's

Fig. 8. *Chessboard Pavilion, Mount Hua, Shenhsi Province.* From People's Art Publishing Co., ed., *The Beauty of Chinese Landscape* (Shanghai: People's Art Publishing Co., 1964).

Fig. 9. *Verdant Mountains* (detail). Handscroll, ink and color on silk. Chiang Shen, ca. 1090–1138, Sung Dynasty. Nelson Gallery-Atkins Museum. 53–49 [23]

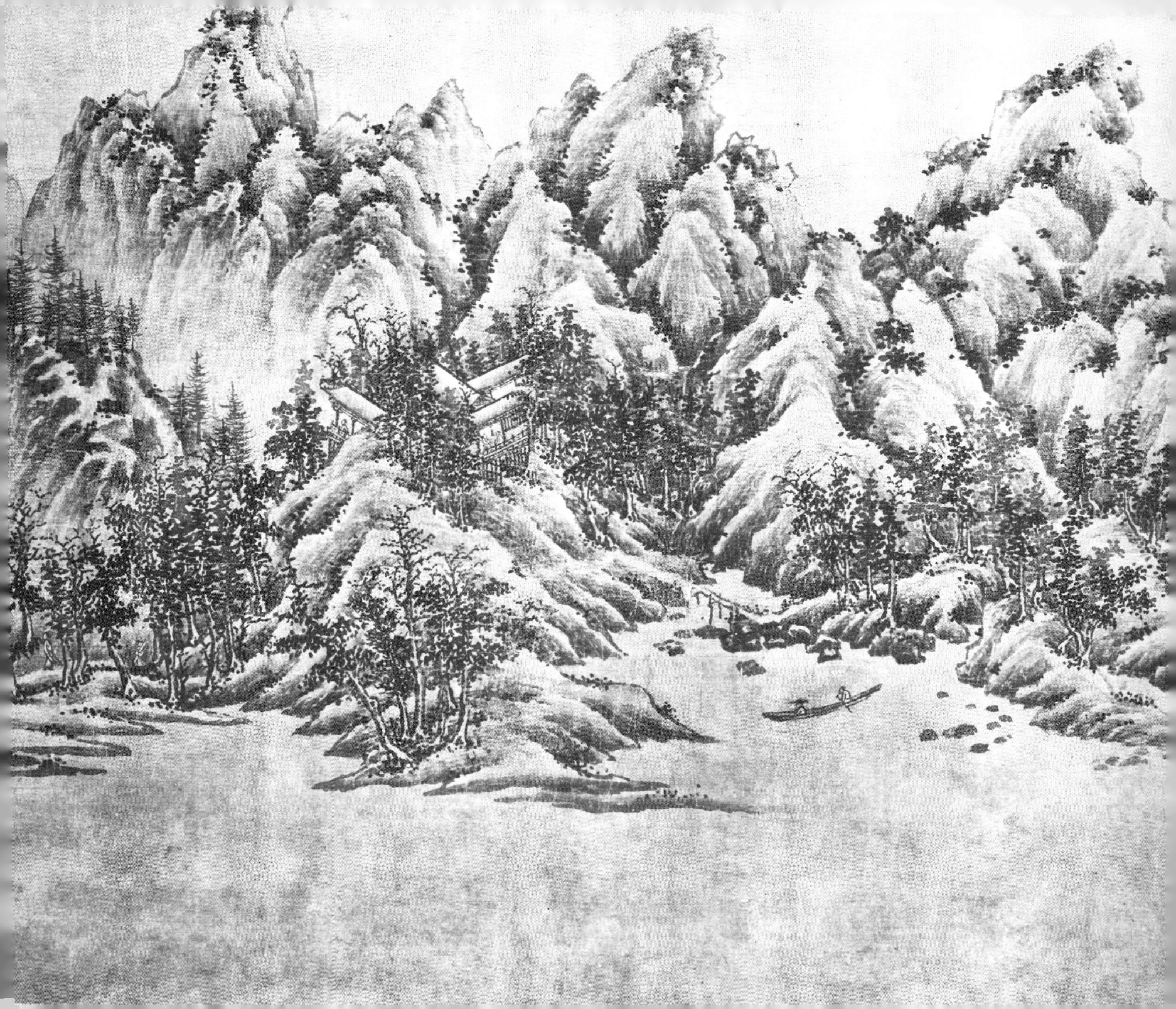

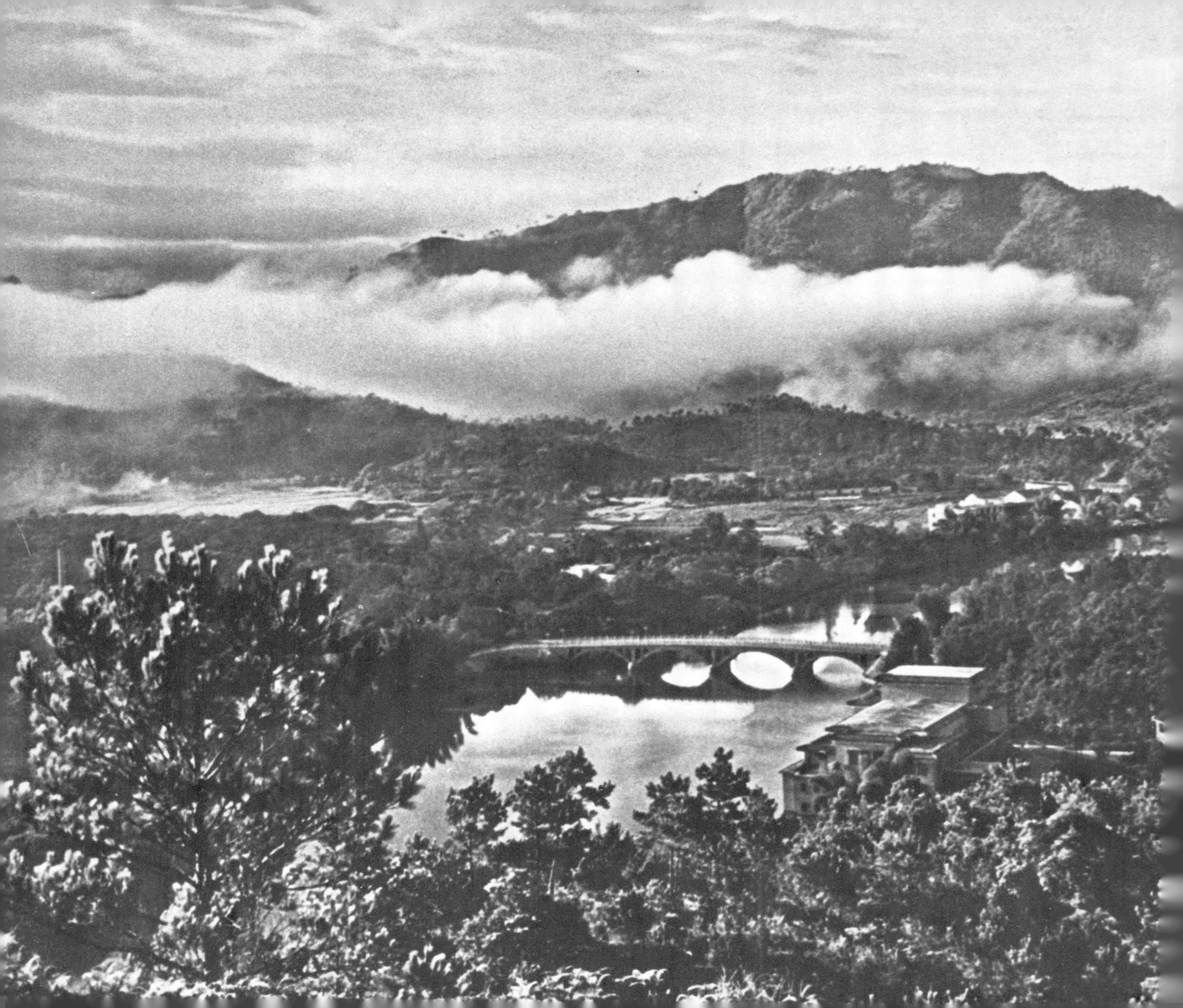

Fig. 10. *Ts'ung-hua Hot Springs, Kuangtung Province.* From People's Art Publishing Co., ed., *The Beauty of Chinese Landscape.* (Shanghai: People's Art Publishing Co., 1964).

Fig. 11. *Cloudy Mountains* (detail). Handscroll, ink and color on silk, dated 1130. Mi Yu-jen, 1072–1151, Southern Sung Dynasty. Purchase from the J. H. Wade Fund. CMA 33.220 [24]

counterpart in the world of painting. Impressed by the overlapping structure and solidarity of similar jagged peaks, the artist defined the mountains and their crevices with brushstrokes of pale watery ink.

Traditionally, southern China was praised in both painting and poetry for its sympathetic climate and rolling mountain ranges softened with lush vegetation. Ts'ung-hua Hot Springs (Fig. 10) in the coastal province of Kuangtung exemplifies southern landscape and is not unlike *Cloudy Mountains* (Fig. 11), a handscroll

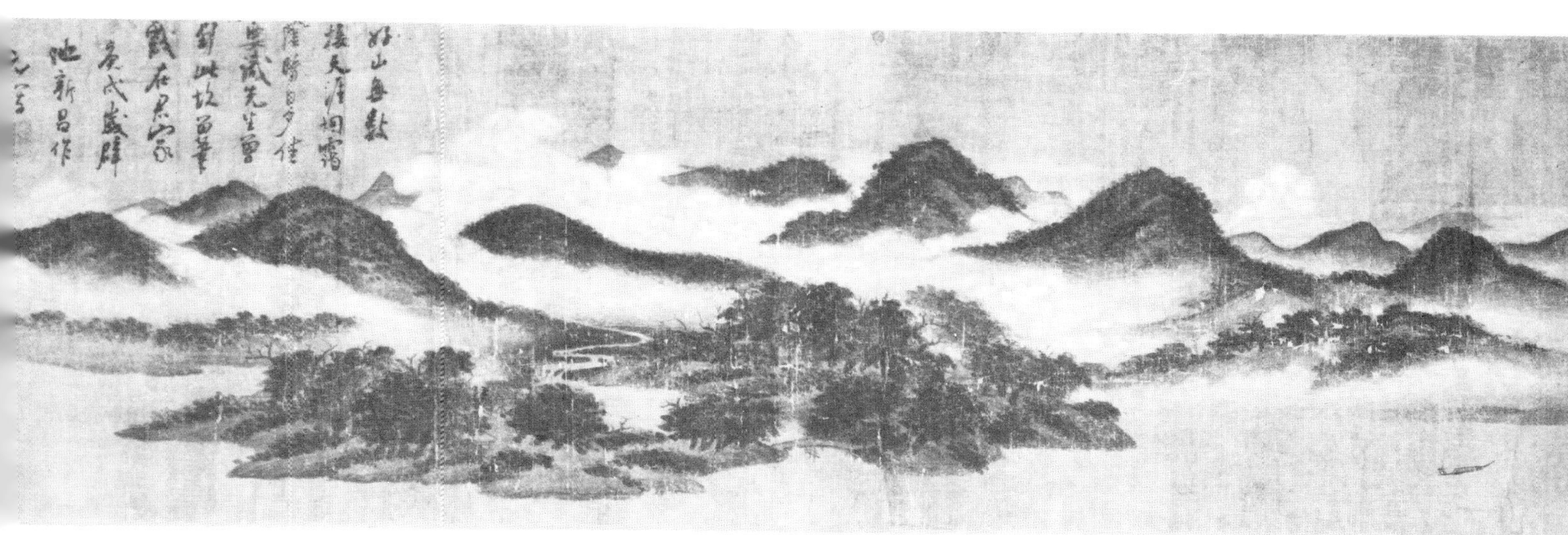

painted in 1130 by Chiang Shen's contemporary Mi Yu-jen. Mi captures the beauties of light and atmosphere in an aerial, panoramic composition of low mountains bordered by an expanse of water. His "dotting" technique rendered the "softer" southern mountainous forms through layering horizontal strokes made with the side of the brush. The artist's inscription at the end of the scroll designates the painting as a gift to an unidentified host.

> *Innumerable are the wonderful mountain peaks*
> * which join the end of the sky,*
> *Clear or cloudy, day or night, the misty atmosphere*
> * is lovely.*
> *To make known that the gentleman has been here,*
> *I am leaving traces of my playful brush at your home.*

Wai-kam Ho, trans.

It is not known whether Chiang traveled to Hua shan or if Mi visited Ts'ung-hua Hot Springs. These sites are merely selected to represent the visible differences between northern and southern topography. It is known, however, that artists frequently journeyed to the countless mountains and rivers famous for their scenic beauties. A unifying practice that transcended historical and regional boundaries, direct observation of natural scenery served as a source of artistic inspiration for all artists. Wang Li, a fourteenth-century artist, aptly affirmed this attitude: "As long as I did not know the form of the Hua Mountain, how could I paint it?"[4] Traveling, a lifelong pleasure, was also essential to the artist's personal, continuous development. It filled him with an innate knowledge of China's notable landscape that could be recalled, even after the passage of many years.

"The beards and the eyebrows of the old masters cannot grow on my face,"[5] declared the eccentric painter Tao-chi (1641–1720), who refused to incorporate the styles of former artists into his own works. Instead of looking at existing paintings for inspiration, Tao-chi, during the later years of his artistic career, largely drew from his experiences while traveling as a young man. He stored mental images of specific geographical locations so that years later he was able to paint, at a friend's request, the Min River during the spring. Similarly, *The Mountain Bends to the Man* (Fig. 12), one of eight album leaves, was created for a friend some ten years after he and Tao-chi hunted for plum blossoms along the Ch'in-huai River near Nanking. His memories of the pleasurable outing were still vivid and fresh even after the passing of a decade.

Freely painted with ink and warm colors, the small painting illustrates a benevolent mountain that seems folded at the center (its crowning trees now suspended upside down) in response to the small, lone figure stretching upward from the boat near the water's edge. This touching encounter demonstrates the communication between man and nature that was firmly entrenched in Chinese society by the philosophical beliefs of both Confucianism and Taoism. This veneration of nature created an atmosphere highly conducive to the growth of landscape painting. Even the rebellious genius Tao-chi, who rejected age-old values, remained steadfast in his reverence and love for nature.

Although few sketches have survived, literary sources disclose that Chinese artists traditionally sketched directly from nature. Ching Hao, one of the

Fig. 12. *The Mountain Bends to the Man* from the album *Reminiscences of the Ch'in-huai River*. Album leaf, ink and color on paper. Tao-ch'i, 1642–1767, Ch'ing Dynasty. Purchase, John L. Severance Fund. CMA 66.31 [238]

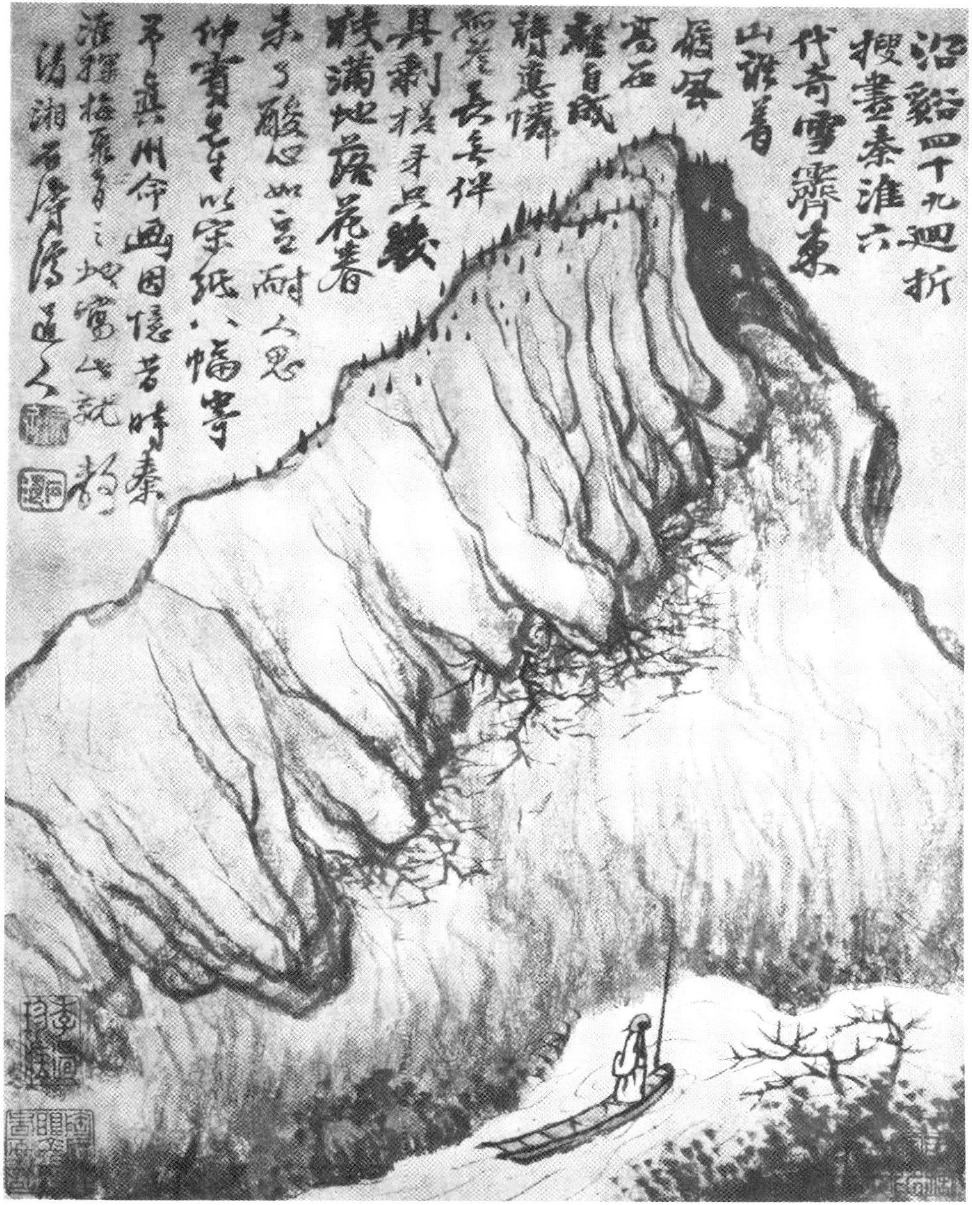

沿谿四十九迴折
搜盡秦淮六
代奇雪霽寒
山誰著
癭瓢
高西
離自咸
詩意僻
兩卷長為伴
其剩揩牙與鞍
枝滿地落花春
赤子酸心如豆耐人思
仰賓老羊以字紙八幅雪
予真州命畫因憶昔時秦
淮擇梅羅雪之地當以就粉
清湘石濤濟道人

earliest northern landscape artists and writers, recorded his fascination with a particularly large, gnarled pine tree. "I walked around and admired it. The next day I returned with my brushes and sketched some [limbs] of the pine tree. After drawing several they seemed real to me."[6] This incident does not appear to be an isolated example nor was sketching a preparatory stage limited to only those tenth- and eleventh-century painters whose intent was the re-creation of nature's forms. It was also a practice among literati artists who viewed painting as an outlet for thoughts and emotions. Huang Kung-wang (1269–1354), celebrated as one of the "Four Great Masters" of the Yüan Dynasty, advised his pupils to always carry a sketching brush in a leather bag so that "when you see in some scenic place a tree that is strange and unique, you can copy its appearance then and there as a record."[7]

The final paintings were, however, created in the artist's studio. The painter always returned to the contemplative, familiar surroundings of his studio where he borrowed images from his sketches but also recalled unrecorded mental impressions. As a composite of his sketches, his paintings described idealized landscapes exhibiting only select types of trees and rocks. Frequently called "type-forms" and pictorial or brush conventions, these forms represented specific types of trees, foliage, rocks, and mountains, and comprised a visual vocabulary for Chinese artists. In developing brush conventions, the artist naturally emphasized the most obvious characteristics of the object as it existed in nature. For example, Li Ch'eng, one of the old masters of Chinese painting, invented the artistic convention that successfully transformed the pine tree (Fig. 16), a common sight throughout China, into a painted image. Simulating the ends of the tree's branches that looked like hooks or the claws of a crab, he contributed the

"crab-claw" tree (Fig. 15) to the ever increasing repertoire of landscape forms.

Successive artistic generations inherited this pictorial vocabulary and added their own brush conventions to the already complex language. By the seventeenth and eighteenth centuries, artists could choose from a variety of suggested forms. It was at this time that China's first instructional manuals or "how-to-paint" books appeared. Used only by beginning artists, these woodblock printed books illustrated those brush conventions or the trees and rocks associated with specific artists. The *Mustard Seed Garden Manual of Painting* (*Chieh Tzu Yüan Hua Chuan*) became the most popular manual among artists living in both China and Japan. Named after the garden of its publisher, Li Yü (1611–1680), it consists of three sections. *Staghorn Branches and Crab-claw Trees* (Fig. 13) is from the first edition of Part I. Printed in 1679, the book explains how to paint trees, rocks, mountains, and people, and includes with each illustration a few descriptive sentences. The obvious pitfall in using such a manual is that it was easy for artists to rely upon it totally, no longer refreshing their mental vocabulary by sketching nature's forms and disregarding the study of actual paintings. Instead of interpreting the spontaneous calligraphic style of an artist's hand, they now copied only harsh, printed outlines created by a printer's knife.

China's first great era of landscape painting occurred some seven hundred years before the printing of the *Mustard Seed Garden Manual of Painting*. The tenth through the thirteenth centuries witnessed the triumph of reality in Chinese painting. Kuo Hsi, an eleventh-century artist, summarized in his treatise *An Essay on Landscape Painting* (*Lin Ch'üan Kao Chih*) the goals of all the great landscapists working during these centuries. Paintings were to inspire in the cultured man a "yearning for forest and stream . . . . How delightful to have a landscape painted by a skilled hand! Without leaving the room, at once he finds himself among the streams and ravines; the cries of birds and monkeys are faintly audible to his senses; light on the hills and reflections on the water, glittering, dazzle his eyes."[8]

To the "lover of forest and stream," landscape paintings served as substitutes for nature. Artists endeavored to capture not only its forms but also its spirit and to inspire in the viewer the same emotional responses from the painting that he would receive if actually experiencing the moment in nature.

Northern Sung artists working during the tenth century and later thirteenth-century Southern Sung artists achieved this same goal through diverse styles. The trend throughout this three-hundred-year period was that of simplification in both painting compositions and brush techniques. Working on large-scale hanging scrolls, the earliest of these masters overwhelmed the viewer with every nuance of the landscape. They described through clear, intricate brushwork the mountains and their severe surfaces as well as each rock and tree. By the thirteenth century, artists selected as their themes only nature's details, vignettes from the much grander setting. Subtle atmospheric touches suggested nature's reality.

Fig. 13. *Staghorn and Crab-claw Trees* from the *Mustard Seed Garden Manual of Painting*. Woodblock print, dated 1679, Ch'ing Dynasty. Nelson Gallery-Atkins Museum.

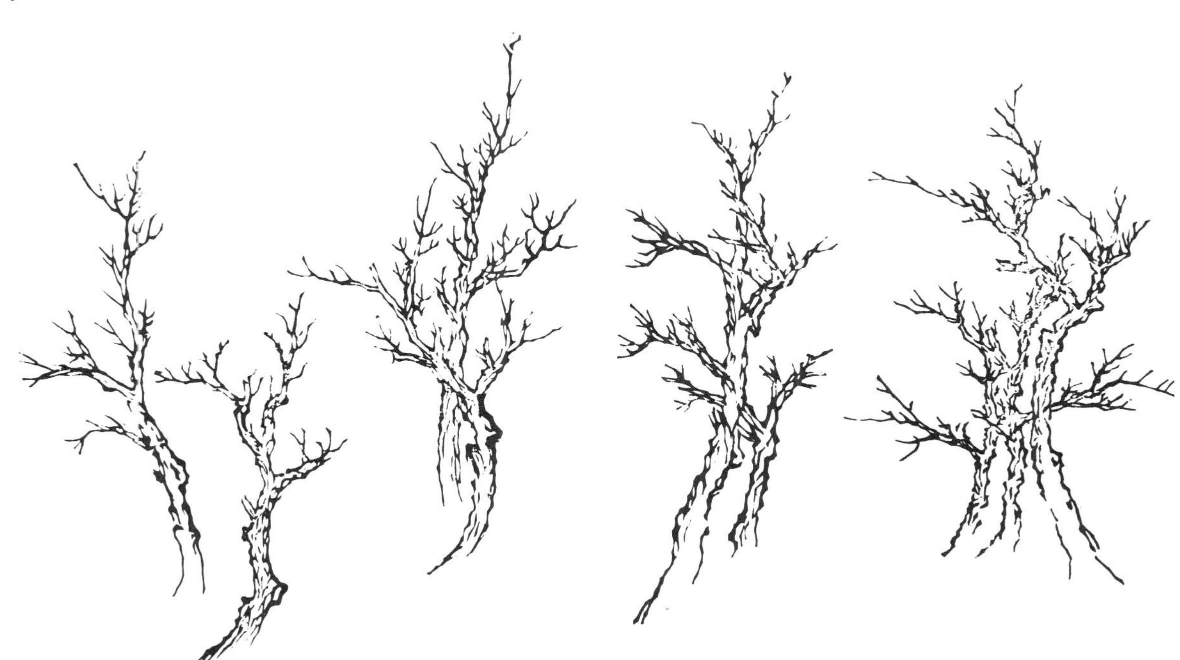

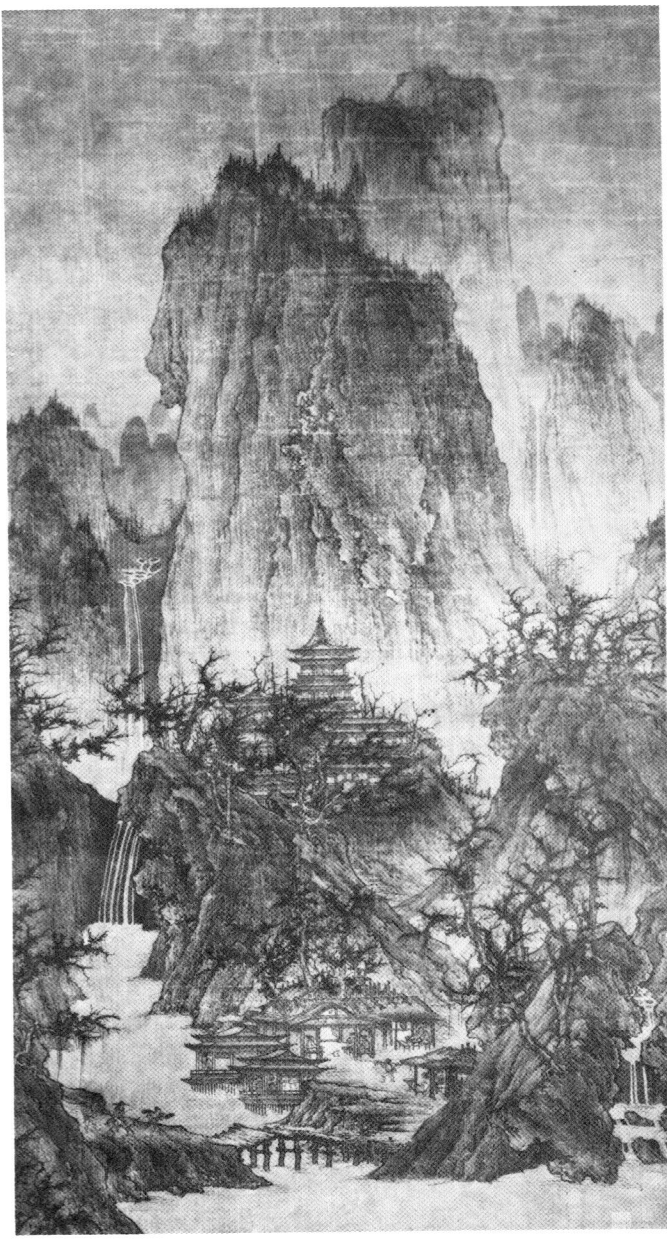

The great landscapist Li Ch'eng (919–967) was the fountainhead of the longest stylistic tradition of Chinese painting. His style is representative of tenth-century Northern Sung landscapes and through his pupil Kuo Hsi and other followers, influenced the artists in his native land as well as those in the neighboring country of Korea. A member of a Confucian family distinguished by six generations of scholar-officials, Li Ch'eng stubbornly refused to serve in a public office and, instead, devoted his life to the art of painting. In the middle of the tenth century he moved from the northern Shantung province to K'aifeng in Honan, the capital of the Northern Sung Dynasty (960–1127) where he became famous for his obstinate refusals to sell his paintings. His favorite theme, wintry landscapes with bare trees, reflects his proud nature and austere temperament.

A Solitary Temple amid Clearing Peaks (Fig. 14), a hanging scroll approximately three and a half feet high painted in ink on silk, is among the few works attributed to Li's hand. The subject, a mountain temple, occupies the center of the painting and symmetrically divides the vertical composition. Behind it rises a towering, cone-shaped mountain that dominates the upper half of the scroll. Near its base, travelers stop for refreshment and conversation in the wineshop identified by the small banner. All narrative elements are dwarfed

Fig. 15. "Crab-claw" Tree (detail) from *A Solitary Temple amid Clearing Peaks*.

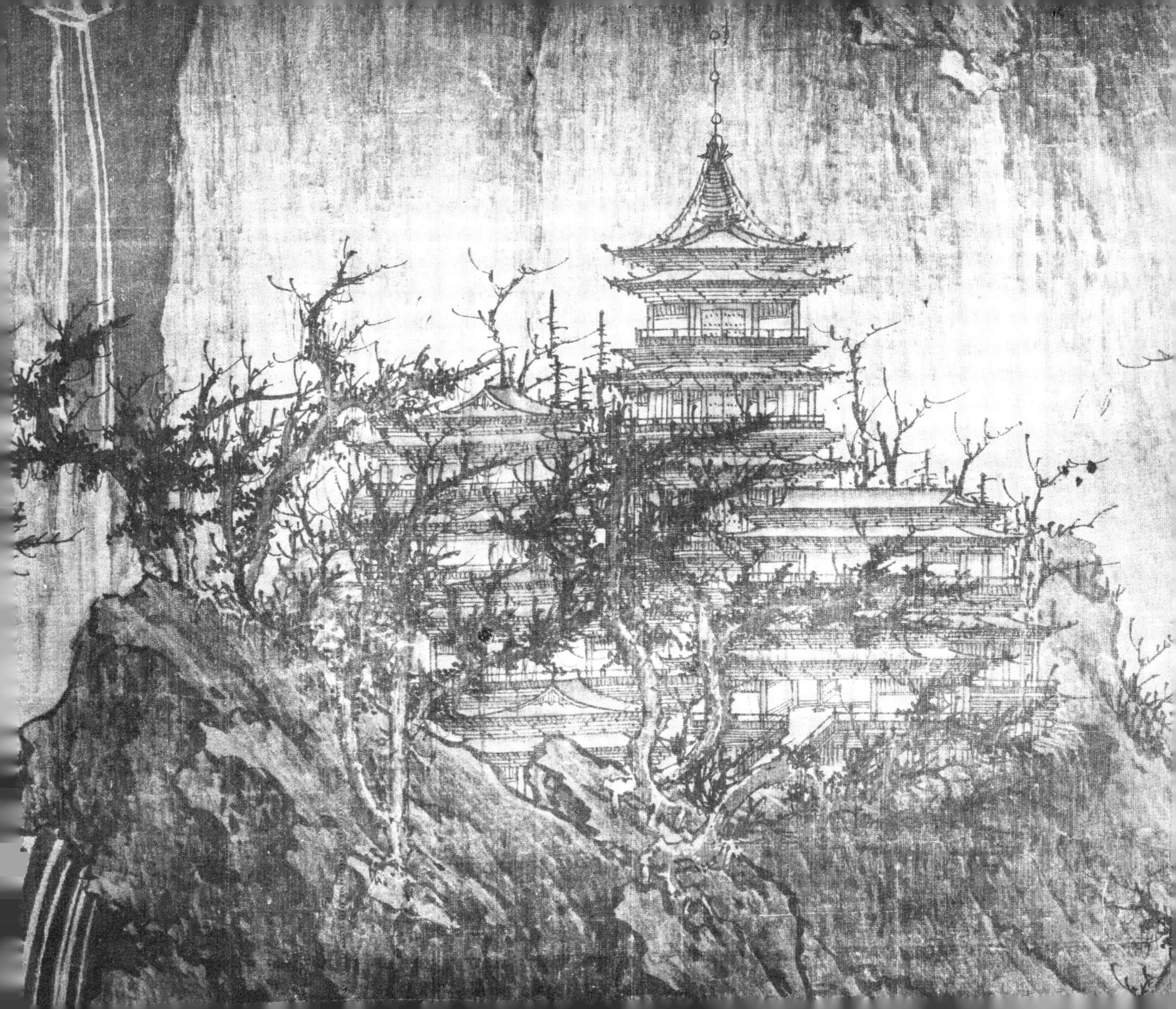

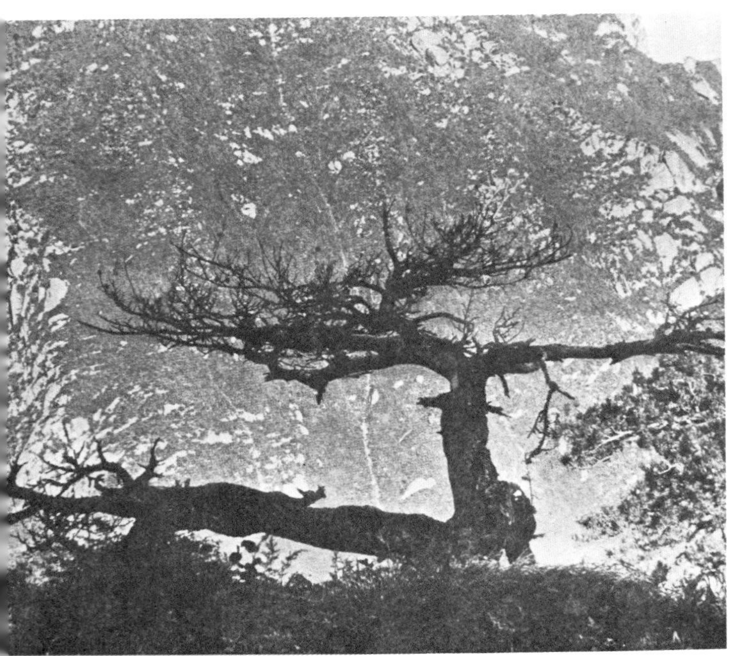

Fig. 16. *Pine Tree*. From Hedda Morrison and Wolfram Eberhard, *Hua Shan: The Taoist Sacred Mountain in West China—Its Scenery, Monasteries and Monks* (Hong Kong: Vetch and Lee, 1974).

by the awe-inspiring landscape. Li Ch'eng captured the grandeur and stateliness of nature through a rationally constructed composition, explicit details, and prodigious brushwork.

Li Ch'eng positions the viewer on a high mountain opposite the river so that he can observe the temple and flanking peak. In contrast to those Western works painted after the Renaissance and composed through the use of scientific perspective, Chinese paintings do not direct the viewer to one specific vantage point. Instead, Eastern compositions—more distinctly divided into foreground, middle ground, and distant views—allow the viewer what has been called a "roving focus": his eyes are free to rest on any part of the landscape

just as they would when confronted with natural scenery. In Li Ch'eng's hanging scroll, for example, the viewer can easily follow the route of approaching travelers at the left: across the bridge, past the wineshop, and up the narrow path to the solemn temple.

Li Ch'eng's composition is tightly organized with overlapping units of rocks and trees that are separate, yet unified through extraordinary brush techniques. Atmospheric effects, indicated by the lightest, unpainted surface of the silk, emphasize the structural divisions of the painting and add clarity to its densely detailed surface. The temple and surrounding pine trees with their reaching branches are silhouetted against the atmospheric band that separates the middle ground from the far distance. Unlike Western landscapes that make use of a definite light source to create dramatic shadows, each form in a Chinese painting is evenly illuminated.

The detail of the "crab-claw" tree flanked by the harsh mountain stone (Fig. 15) is only one indication of the complex, descriptive brushwork in Li's commanding work. The "crab-claw" branches of the tree were created by confident, hooklike strokes, and each craggy formation is outlined with a sharp, black line. The modeling, or texturing, of the creviced surface was achieved through layers of long brushstrokes and a stippling brush technique that provided triangular im-

Fig. 17. *Ramblers over a Windy Stream*. Album leaf, ink on silk. Lo Chih-ch'uan, died before 1330, Yüan Dynasty. Gift of The John Huntington Art and Polytechnic Trust. CMA 15.536 [101]

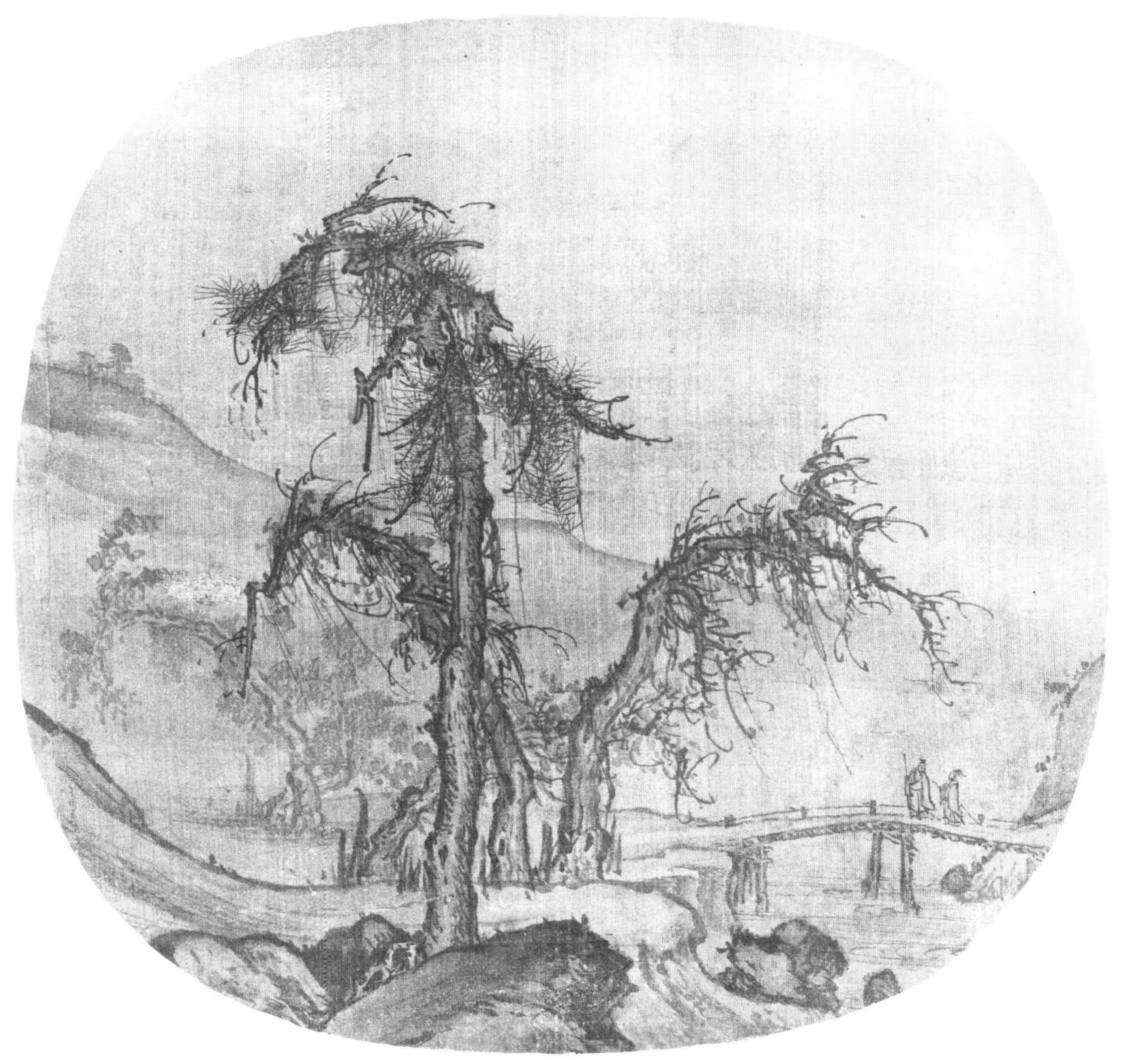

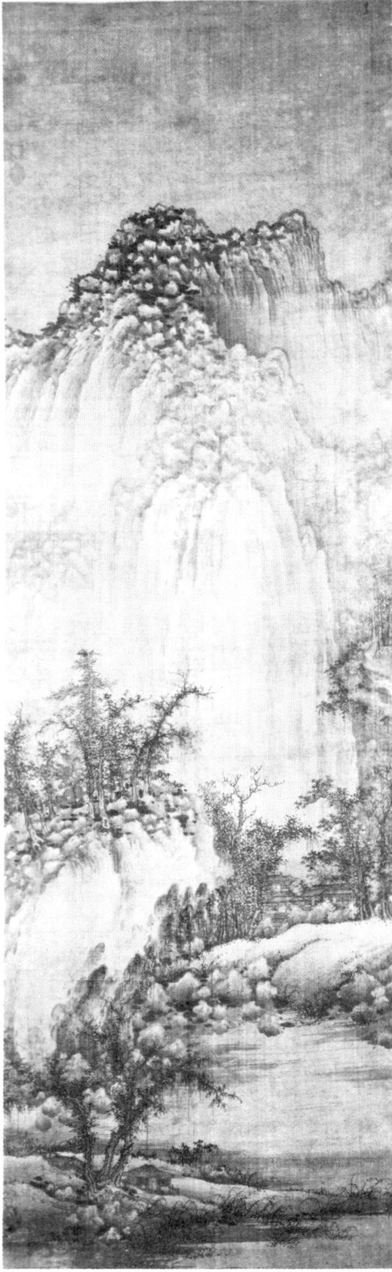

Fig. 18. *Buddhist Retreat by Stream and Mountain.* Hanging scroll, ink on silk. Chü-jan, active ca. 960–985, Northern Sung Dynasty. Gift of Katharine Holden Thayer. CMA 59.348 [11]

pressions. These intricate, laborious painting techniques impart a sense of solidity and authenticity to the monumental landscape.

Le Ch'eng's trademark, the "crab-claw" tree, populated many a landscape over the next nine hundred years. His stylistic tradition, named the Li-Kuo school from the combination of his surname with that of Kuo Hsi, flourished in northern and southern China during the twelfth and thirteenth centuries. As time progressed, the pine—now a symbol of the Li-Kuo school—was no longer subordinate in the landscape setting but achieved distinction as a theme independent of the monumental mountainous scenery. In his album leaf *Ramblers over a Windy Stream* (Fig. 17), the obscure fourteenth-century artist Lo Chih-ch'uan cast the pine tree in a simplified setting; his background mountains are reduced to a simple line with minimal shading.

Buddhist Retreat by Stream and Mountain (Fig. 18), a large hanging scroll by another tenth-century master, Chü-jan, is thought to be the fifth and only remaining panel from an original set of six paintings entitled *Distant Peaks Floating in the Mist.* Although similar in theme to Li Ch'eng's austere landscape, the Buddhist complex nestled at the base of the looming mountain is more intimately related to the monk Chü-jan.

Very little is known about Chü-jan's personal life. A native of Nanking, Chiangsu, he moved north in 975 to

Fig. 19. *Buddhist Retreat by Stream and Mountain* (detail).

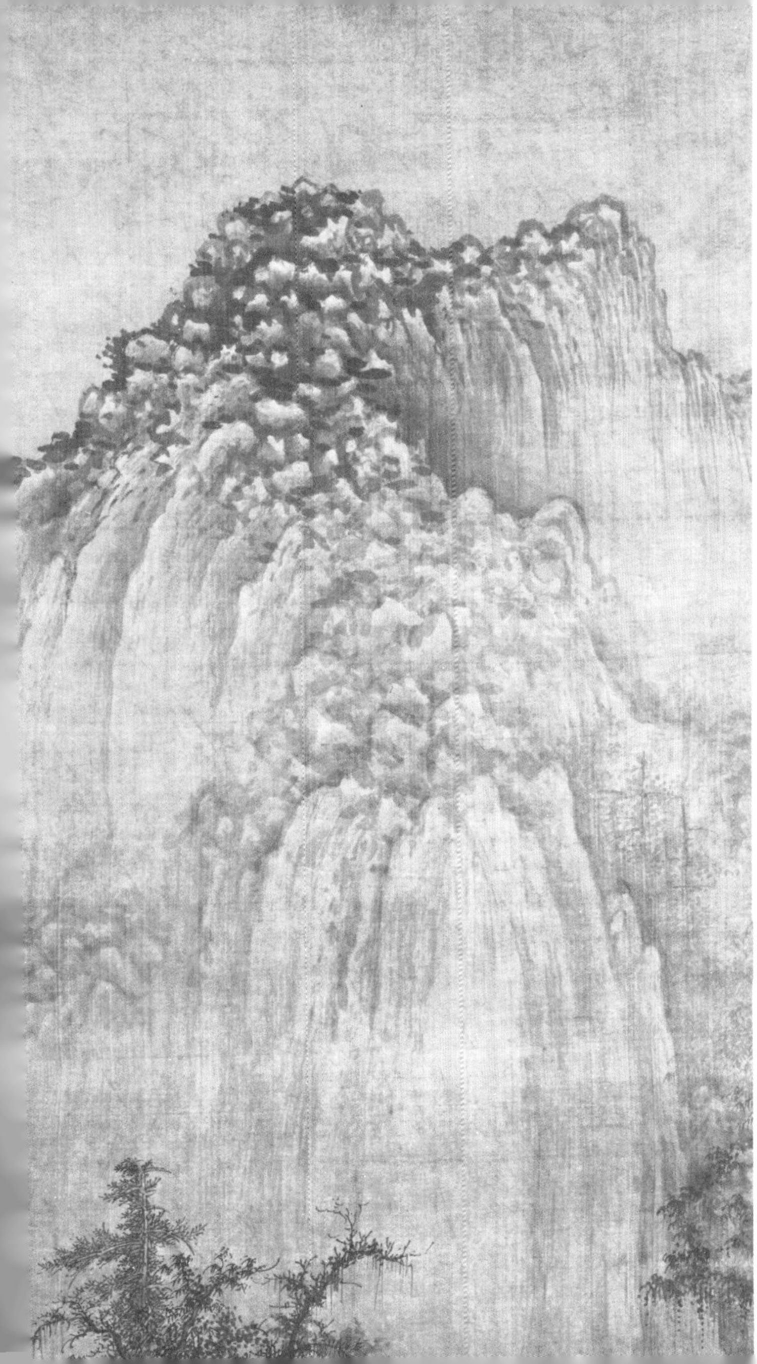

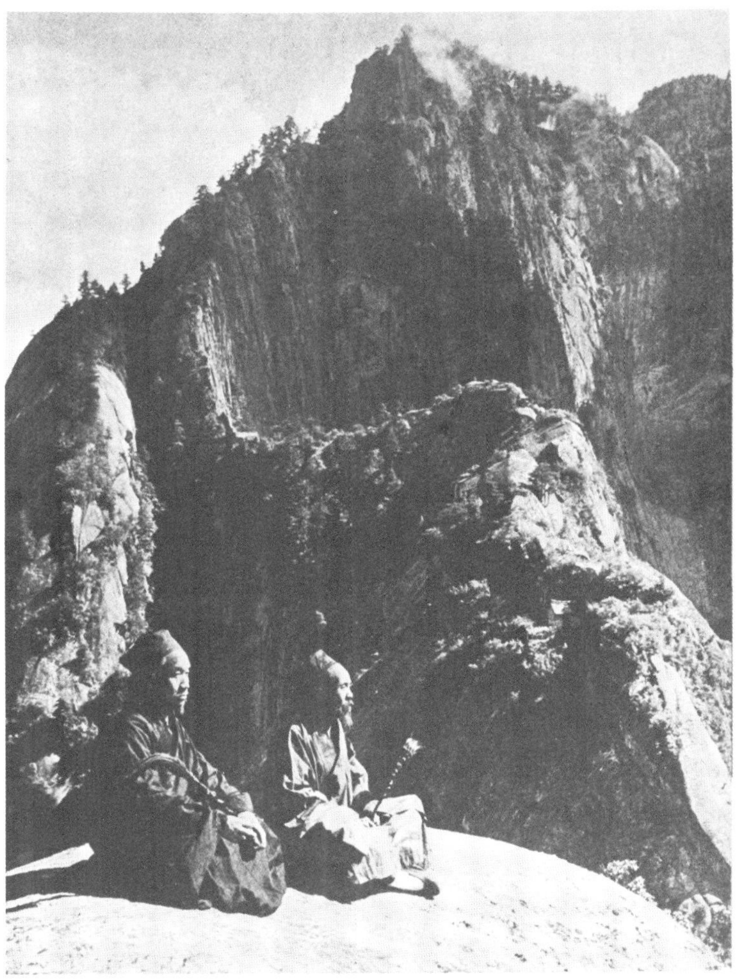

Fig. 20. *Mount Hua*. From Hedda Morrison and Wolfram Eberhard, *Hua Shan: The Taoist Sacred Mountain in West China —Its Scenery, Monasteries and Monks* (Hong Kong: Vetch and Lee, 1974).

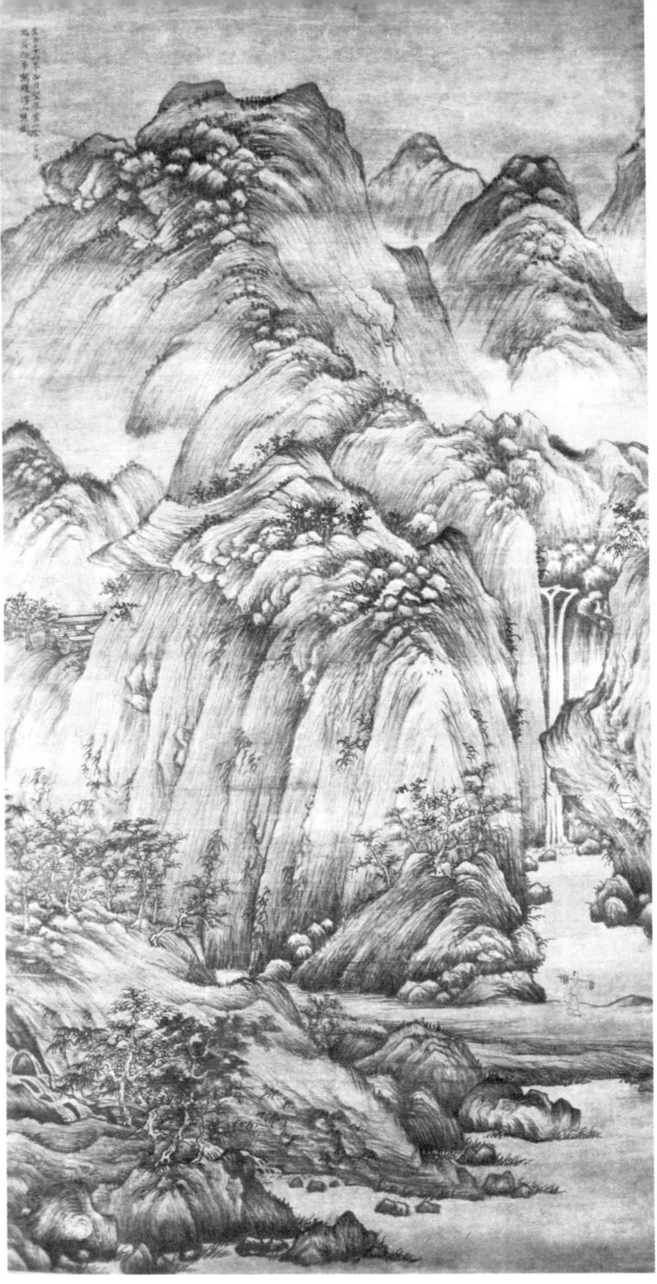

the Northern Sung capital, K'aifeng, where he entered the K'ai-yüan monastery. Favored by leading artistic circles, his paintings were added to the collection of the ruling family; the twelfth-century catalog of the imperial collection includes one hundred twenty works by Chü-jan. Today, there remain less than five paintings attributed to his hand. Literary documentation and stylistic analysis confirm *Buddhist Retreat by Stream and Mountain* to be one of Chü-jan's masterpieces.

Chü-jan organized his vertical composition formally into foreground, middle ground, and far distance. Narrative elements — foreground pavilions and the Buddhist retreat — are sheltered by leaning pines and the shadowy mountain dominating the far distance. The distinctive **S** curve of the mountain's ridges (Fig. 19) emulates natural prototypes and is very similar to geological formations of the Hua shan mountain range (Fig. 20). Chü-jan transformed the boulders that cap this undulating form into brush conventions called "alum-head" stones. Enlivened by darker ink accents, the "alum-head" stones became Chü-jan's personal insignia.

Chü-jan's soft amorphous brushwork subtly defining the creviced mountains illustrates a delicate balance between painted, abstract forms and pictorial images descriptive of the natural world. Later artists such as Ch'en Ju-yen (active ca. 1340–1370), who imitated Ch'en's style in the hanging scroll *The Woodcutter of Mount Lo-fou* (Fig. 21), disturbed this fragile equilibrium by overemphasizing the artist's brush conventions. Ch'en Ju-yen crystallized Chü-jan's soft brushwork into

Fig. 21. *The Woodcutter of Mount Lo-fou.* Hanging scroll, ink on silk, dated 1366. Ch'en Ju-yen, ca. 1331–before 1371, Yüan Dynasty. Mr. and Mrs. A. Dean Perry Collection. [113]

dark, outlining strokes. The mountain's gently descending planes were tranposed into an accordion-like structure. The "alum-head" stones, individually outlined and modeled, are no longer an integral part of the mountain but remain independent, separate units.

A later observer inscribed this scroll, painted in 1366, and suggested that Ch'en Ju-yen's woodcutter represents Ko Hung, a famous Taoist alchemist who wrote the first text of Taoist terminology. In his impoverished youth, he is known to have chopped firewood in order to buy the ink and paper necessary for his studies.

Although in the following generations Chü-jan's and Li Ch'eng's diverse styles became widely known throughout China, during the tenth century they were basically regional styles, with origins in northern and southern China. Li Ch'eng's explicitly detailed landscape—each form outlined with dark brushstrokes and modeled through overlapping strokes and washes—epitomizes the style prevalent in northern China. In contrast, Chü-jan created his landscape using an implicit, summary style. He contoured and modeled the mountain's curving ridges with a pale, more fluid ink and a single type of brushstroke, the "hemp-fiber" stroke.

Tung Yüan (907–968), an artist and minor official of the imperial parks who like Chü-jan also lived in Nanking, originated this "southern" style. Still a young man when Tung died, Chü-jan adopted the older artist's style during the formative years of his artistic career. Tung Yüan and Chü-jan, the founders of the Tung-Chü landscape tradition, are considered the stylistic ancestors of such noted literati as Wu Chen (see Cover). Literati painters praised their use of pale, "bland" ink with only slight tonal variations and the simplicity of their brushwork.

Chü-jan moved to K'aifeng only eight years after Li Ch'eng's death. No doubt Li's works were still visible in select collections throughout the capital. The groupings of "crab-claw" trees in the foreground as well as the tree with "staghorn" branches (see also Fig. 13) silhouetted against the base of the mountain demonstrate Chü-jan's familiarity with Li Ch'eng's paintings. Rather than simply copying this motif, Chü-jan integrated it into his own personal, creative style—a distinctive characteristic of a great artist.

Approximately one and a half centuries after Chü-jan's death, invading Chin Tartars swept down from China's northern borders, sacked the capital of K'aifeng, and drove the court south to Hangchou, Chechiang. This city, singled out by Marco Polo in the thirteenth century as one of the most beautiful in the world, became the new capital of the Southern Sung Dynasty. Drastically reduced in size, the Chinese empire made peace with their violent neighbors and settled to enjoy the beauty and pleasant climate of southeastern China.

Attempting to revive the cultural and artistic brilliance of his father's court in K'aifeng, the new emperor, Kao-tsung (reigned 1127–1162), lost little time in reassembling the Painting Academy. One member of the Northern Sung Painting Academy, Li T'ang (ca. 1050–1130), was found selling his paintings in a marketplace. Given the honorary title of Painter-in-Attendance, he became the leading master of the new academy. Ma Yüan (active ca. 1184–1225) was foremost among his followers.

Bamboo and Ducks by a Rushing Stream (Fig. 22), a hanging scroll probably from an original set of four illustrating seasonal themes, was painted by Ma Yüan, who signed his name beneath the stalks of bamboo.

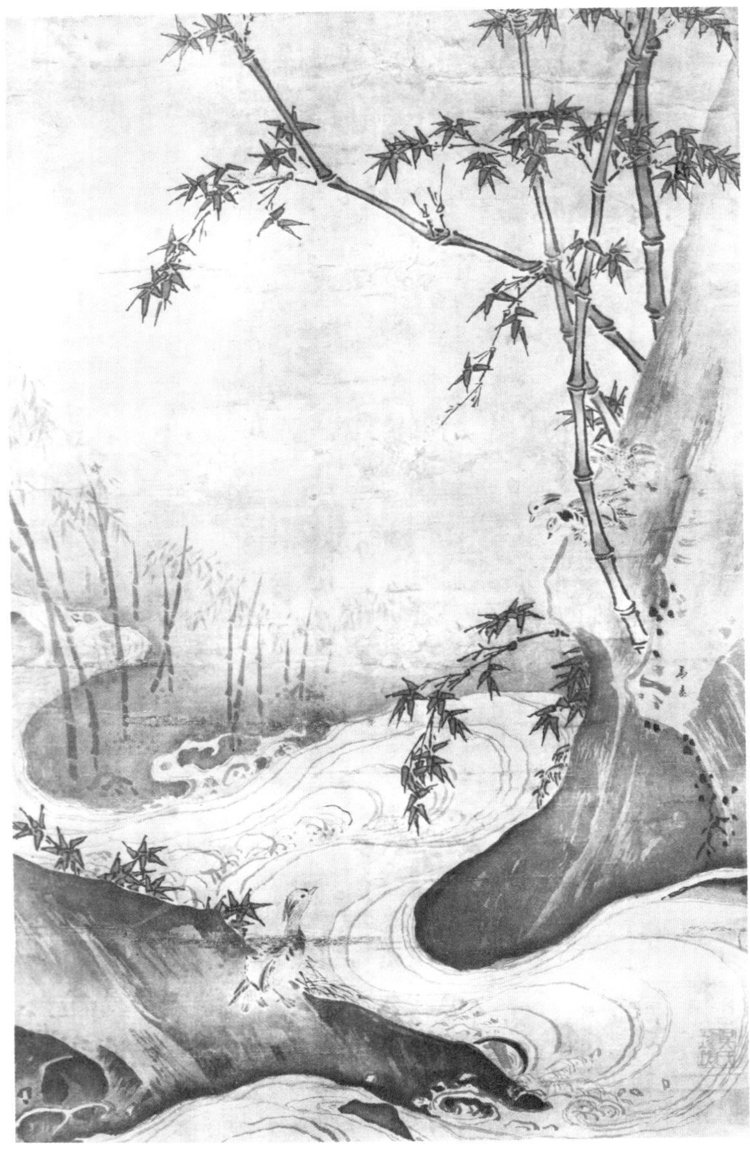

Fig. 22. *Bamboo and Ducks by a Rushing Stream*. Hanging scroll, ink and color on silk. Ma Yüan, active ca. 1190 – 1224, Southern Sung Dynasty. Purchase from the J. H. Wade Fund. CMA 67.145 [54]

The young bamboo plants arch over a swelling, rushing stream that separates the lone duck from his three companions. This painting of birds in the spring complements another hanging scroll of birds in winter. *Egrets in a Snow Landscape* (in the collection of the National Palace Museum, Taipei, Taiwan) and *Bamboo and Ducks by a Rushing Stream* are the only compositions remaining from the original set.

Ma Yüan's work is typical of Southern Sung Academy paintings in theme, composition, and brush techniques. Unlike the Northern Sung landscapists who strove to capture the completeness and power of nature through carefully detailed and rationally constructed compositions, Southern Sung artists focused on select elements of the natural scenery. Ma Yüan chose as his theme only a bamboo grove, a stream, and four ducks.

Asymmetrically composed, Ma Yüan's painting is weighted at the right side by a bamboo-studded embankment. The sinuously curving stream leads the viewer to a distant, misty bamboo grove. While Northern Sung artists strove to create solid and believable forms, Southern Sung artists experimented with atmospheric perspective. Through subtle nuances such as the pale brushstrokes that indicate bamboo leaves, Ma Yüan suggests the existence of a continuous space.

In contrast to Li Ch'eng's intricate texturing of stony surfaces through layers of ink wash and brushstrokes, Ma Yüan defined the character of the stream's rocky

Fig. 23. ''Axe-cut'' Brushstroke (detail) from *Bamboo and Ducks by a Rushing Stream.*

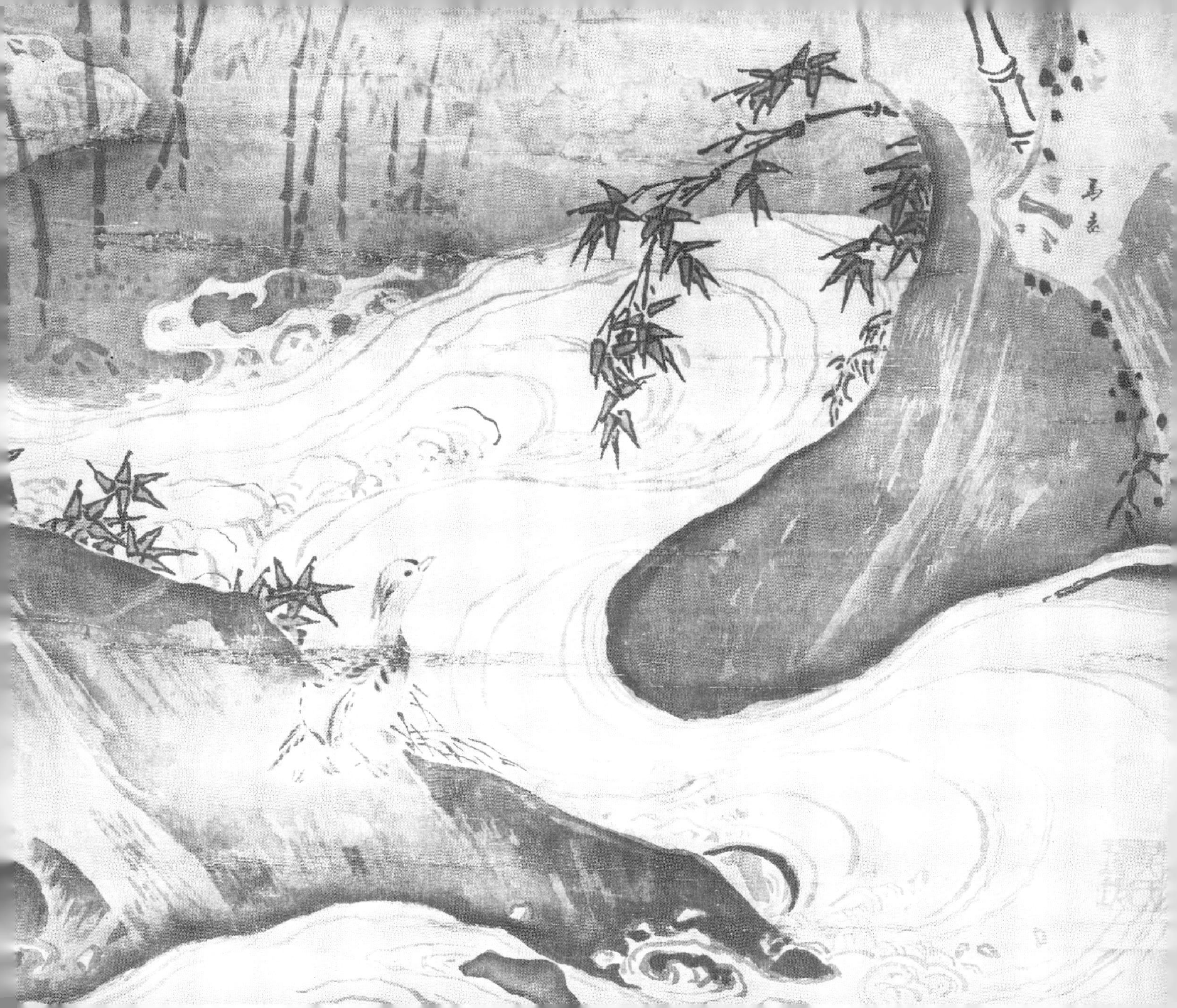

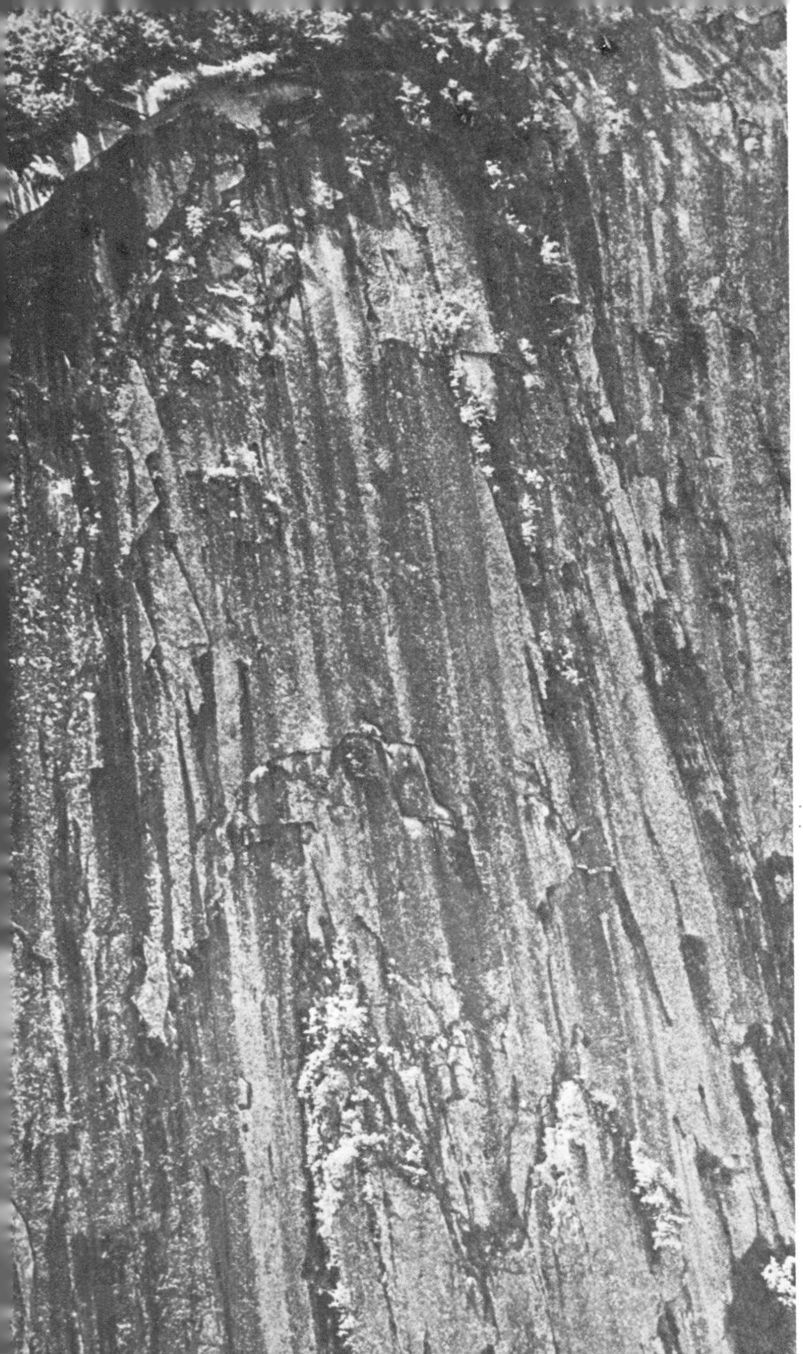

shores through one simple brushstroke, the "axe-cut" stroke (Fig. 23). Positioned adjacent to Ma Yüan's signature and on the narrow shoal extending at the opposite side of the stream, the stroke resembles the mark left by an axe when chopping wood. It ingeniously describes the sharp cleavages of stone discernable in the natural environment (Fig. 24). Originated by Li T'ang, the stroke is made through "laying the brush on its side and dragging it down, using the flat side of the brush. The stroke is straight at the top and ends in irregular points as the ink runs dry or the brush is lifted."[9]

Although the Painting Academy ended with the 1279 Mongolian invasions, it was briefly revived in Peking during the fifteenth century by the early emperors of the Ming Dynasty. A conservative, reactionary spirit characterized the artistic and political circles of this eventful era that marked a return to native rule after the foreign-dominated Yüan Dynasty. Tai Chin (1388–1462), a Painter-in-Attendance of the new academy and the founder of the Che school, looked to Ma Yüan and his contemporaries for stylistic inspiration.

As a court artist, Tai Chin painted official portraits, recorded important occasions, and prepared large hanging scrolls to decorate official quarters. Tai Chin's painting, *The Hermit Hsü Yu Resting by a Stream* (Fig. 25), probably served this latter purpose and illustrates a Confucian paragon, a theme appropriate for the halls of officialdom.

Fig. 24. *Rock Wall of the Great Crater, Mount Hua.* From Hedda Morrison and Wolfram Eberhard, *Hua Shan: The Taoist Sacred Mountain in West China — Its Scenery, Monasteries and Monks* (Hong Kong: Vetch and Lee, 1974).

Hsü Yu, the focal point of the composition, wears a shepherd's costume and sits on a broad plateau with his walking staff nearby. This legendary hermit who lived during the third millenrium BC exemplifies the Confucian principle of choosing to serve the government only at the right time and under the right circumstances. Hsü Yu refused to succeed Emperor Yao as China's ruler and, instead, withdrew to the mountains where he lived as a recluse. Tai Chin's faithfulness to Ma Yüan's style is obvious. The angular pine, foreground rock, and distant mountains — accented with dark "axe-cut" strokes — dominate the left half of the asymmetrical composition.

The forced migration of the northern Chinese court to the south during the early twelfth century, in turn, caused a mass relocation of China's educated elite, the literati. The area below the Yangtze River around Hangchou, Suchou, and Nanking remained from that time until well into the nineteenth century one of China's most prosperous regions and the creative center of Chinese painting. Removed from the Mongol court, literati painters flourished in this geographical location. They, too, continued to seek inspiration from both nature's forms and paintings of the old masters. But in the new cultural climate they ushered in a new epoch of Chinese painting.

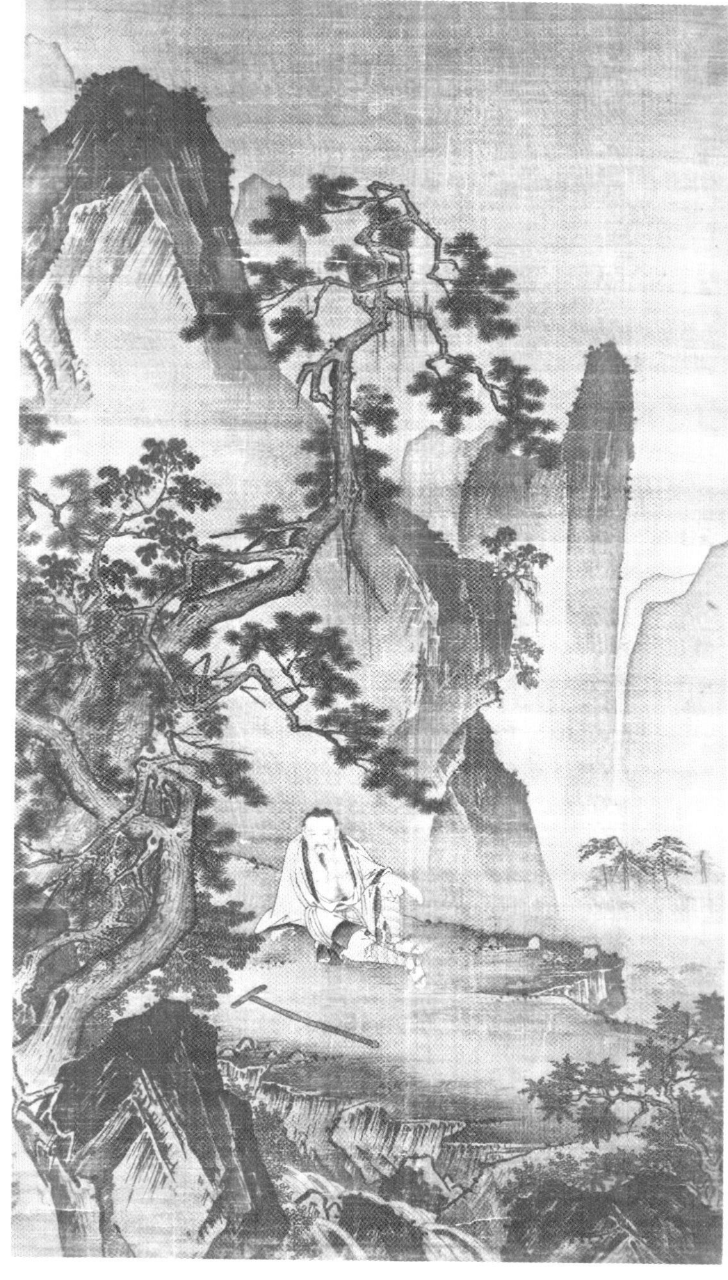

Fig. 25. *Hermit Hsü Yu Resting by a Stream*. Hanging scroll, ink and color on silk. Tai Chin, 1388–1462, Ming Dynasty. Purchase, John L. Severance Fund. CMA 74.45 [134]

Literati Painting: The Scholar's Tradition

Chinese literati painters can be characterized as a garrulous coterie of cultured gentlemen who exchanged paintings, poetry, and cups of wine at jovial gatherings. They are just as often described as aloof, detached recluses who preferred a solitary existence interrupted only occasionally by visits from intimate friends. Paradoxically, these assessments are as dependent upon the individual as upon the political and social circumstances of the particular era in which they lived. Numerous paintings still in existence record both the congenial and remote natures of the literati (Fig. 26 and Cover).

The literati, or scholar-amateur painters, were first and foremost Confucian scholars, men cultivated through the study of Chinese classical literature and history. Their lifelong pursuit and only suitable occupation was that of a government official. Bureaucratic positions within the ruling administration, both important and petty, were awarded primarily on the basis of the strenuous civil service examinations that tested the competitor's creative, literary skills and his knowledge of the Five Chinese Classics. Originating in ancient China from the Shang (sixteenth century–1045 BC) through the Han dynasties, these five classics include the *Book of Changes (I-ching)*, *Book of History (Shu-ching)*, *Book of Poetry (Shih-ching)*, *Ritual (Li-chi)*, and the *Spring and Autumn Annals (Ch'un-ch'iu)*. Study of these texts was essential to the philosophy of Confucianism that stressed traditional ethical and moral standards for man and society. It enabled the literati to develop in themselves the virtue and wisdom of China's noble past by studying the Confucian classics. As the intelligentsia of traditional China, the literati, or *wen-jen*, were superior in intellect, education, and social status. Their moral responsibility was to bring morality and order to the political state.

Proud of their years of study, self-cultivation, and public service, these scholars were enthusiastic painters. For them, painting was considered only a pastime, a polite art of amateurs to be enjoyed at leisure. While the literati tradition can be traced as early as the T'ang and Northern Sung dynasties, it only developed into a significant, predominant element of Chinese painting later, during the fourteenth century of the Mongol-ruled Yüan Dynasty. Within this short time the literati revolutionized Chinese painting, emphasizing expressive brush techniques rather than the total pictorial image and elevating painting to the level of the other venerated arts — calligraphy, poetry, and music.

The designation scholar-amateur was further meant to distinguish these artists from the court and professional painters who painted as a means of livelihood and flourished under the patronage of aesthetically minded emperors and wealthy, landed gentry. During the Sung Dynasty, court painters increased in number and prestige and became leading artists. Serving in the Academy of Painting, these artists, like the preceding generations of painters, strove to achieve realistic, faithful recordings of nature's models. Their paintings of birds and flowers or the misty, romantic landscapes that surrounded the Southern Sung capital of Hangchou were meant to "look like" the actual object or scene represented. Scholar-amateur painters, on the other hand, were more concerned with expressive brushwork than representational fidelity. They believed their works to be personal forms of communication, revealing an individual's noble character and integrity. They chided the professional artists, categorizing them as mere "artisans" who painted for financial stability rather than to express inner thoughts and feelings. In contrast to the colorful, decorative paintings of the professional artists, the literati favored the simplicity of monochromatic ink tones and often purposefully imbued their works with a slight awkwardness and an air of naivité. In accompanying inscriptions, they labeled their works mere "ink plays." Disdainful of commercialism, the literati prided themselves on painting only for their own pleasure and that of their friends. When an unknowing admirer of the eleventh-century bamboo artist Wen T'ung asked him for a painting and brought him a gift of silk on which to paint, the indignant Wen replied, "I'll make it into socks!"[10] Similarly, the greatest calligrapher of the thirteenth century and one of the founders of the literati movement, Chao Meng-fu, copied for a Buddhist priest the popular holy text, the "Heart" Sutra, in exchange for a very modest remuneration — a cup of tea (see Fig. 41).

The literati were celebrators of antiquity. Entrenched in the past, they "intellectualized" Chinese painting through sometimes overt but more often subtle references to past literary and artistic styles. They painted through both visual and written symbols that could be interpreted on different levels. Only individuals of equal social status and education could understand their obtuse references and fully appreciate their clev-

erness and ingenuity. Artistic companionships and cliques were extremely important in this highly personal art and, despite the complexity of routine bureaucratic duties, there were always free hours to spend in the company of compatible friends. They met at either impromptu, informal affairs that included only a few close friends or at much larger events, usually staged in rural, scenic settings to celebrate a festival, birthday, or holiday. For entertainment these gentlemen composed poetry, painted, and listened to musical performances on the Chinese lute. Their paintings, frequently accompanied by complementary inscriptions, were also exchanged as tokens of friendship or mementoes of the occasion. Like many of the antiquarian interests of the participants, these gatherings were rooted in China's historic past. These scholarly gatherings occurred more frequently in the Ming and Ch'ing (1644–1911) dynasties and became suitable topics for painting.

The oldest and most popular literati gathering, the *Purification at the Orchid Pavilion* (Fig. 26), was illustrated in 1671 by Fan I (active ca. 1658–1671), an artist living in the vicinity of Nanking, Chiangsu. With origins in the Spring Purification Festival that welcomed the arrival of the new season, this particular theme records the fourth-century gathering of forty-two scholarly colleagues at Wang Hsi-chih's (AD 321–379) Orchid Pavilion. Servant youths busily set cups of wine afloat in a nearby stream while their masters relaxed along the banks within easy reach of the drifting wine cups. During a poetry contest those scholars who failed to finish their verses suffered penalties: they were required to gulp extra cups of wine. What may seem to be a peculiar penalty was not totally without rationality: the Chinese knew "spirits" to be an inspiring elixir.

First illustrated in the eleventh century, the *Purification of the Orchid Pavilion* had been a favorite theme

Fig. 26. *Purification at the Orchid Pavilion* (detail). Handscroll, ink and color on silk, dated 1671. Fan I, active ca. 1658–1671, Ch'ing Dynasty. Gift of the Junior Council of The Cleveland Museum of Art and Mrs. Wai-kam Ho in the name of the Junior Council. CMA 77.47 [218]

among Chinese artists for six hundred years before Fan I painted his handscroll (Fig. 26). He depicted the dignified participants with such decorum that one can only conclude they are either very competent, strait-laced poets or the afternoon is yet young and the amount of spirits consumed has not yet taken effect. By the seventeenth century, artists rendering this theme emphasized the landscape setting rather than the indi-vidual, historic scholars. Fan I painted the varied trees

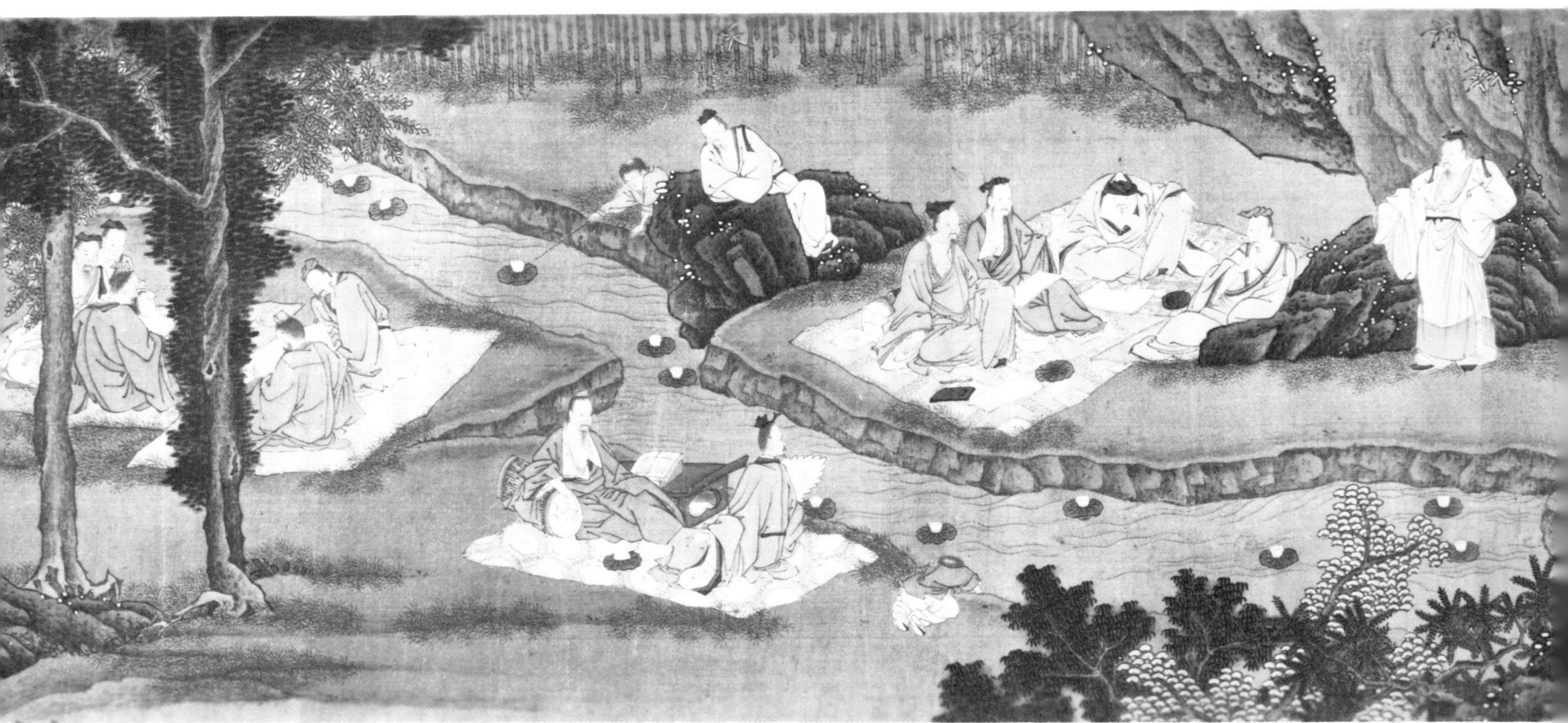

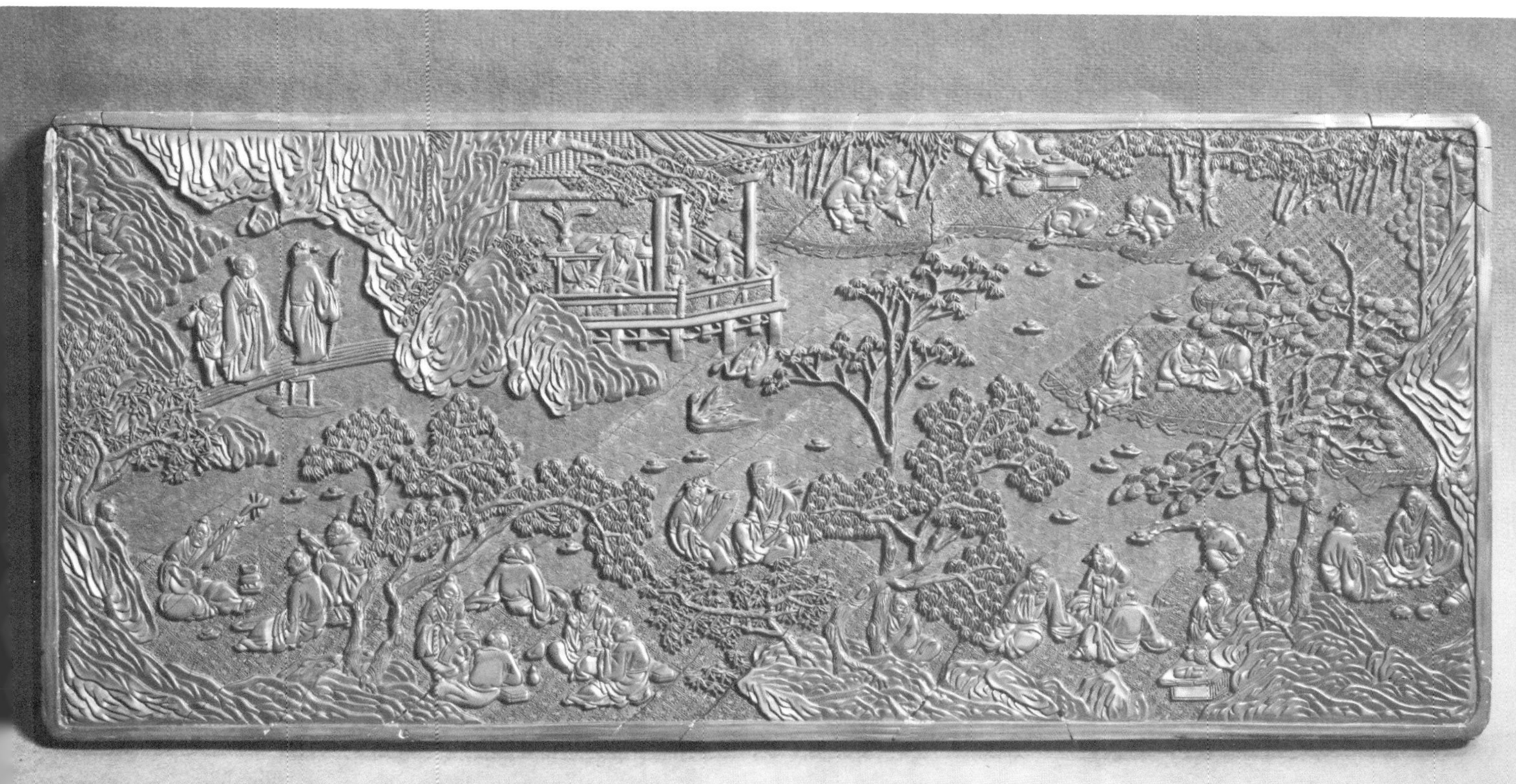

with the same precise brushwork as the figures that illustrate the narrative theme. His use of the bright mineral colors — azurite blue and malachite green — recalls an older painting style popular during the T'ang Dynasty and reinforces this antique theme. Not limited to painting, the theme became a decorative motif used in other media, as illustrated in a sixteenth-century lacquer panel (Fig. 27).

Fig. 27. *Purification at the Orchid Pavilion*. Lacquer, carved cinnabar. Ming Dynasty, ca. 1500. Purchase, Andrew R. and Martha Holden Jennings Fund. CMA 74.72

43

The wine-imbibing scholars carried with them on these rustic gatherings their portable collections — books, handscrolls, folding fans, and albums of calligraphy and painting. These painting formats were more intimate than the large, hanging scrolls and were meant to be held in laps or put on a low table and viewed like a book. The resemblance of these scrolls to books, the scholar's constant companions, may be one reason they were so popular among the literati. Another reason might be that these small formats were made of paper. In general, the literati preferred to paint on paper instead of the finely woven silk favored by the professional and court painters. Paper allowed them the greater flexibility of brush techniques that produced abstract, expressive qualities in their paintings.

Folding fans, such as *Banana Trees* (Fig. 28) by the eighteenth-century artist Lo P'ing (1733–1799), could be painted quickly and were often exchanged as gifts

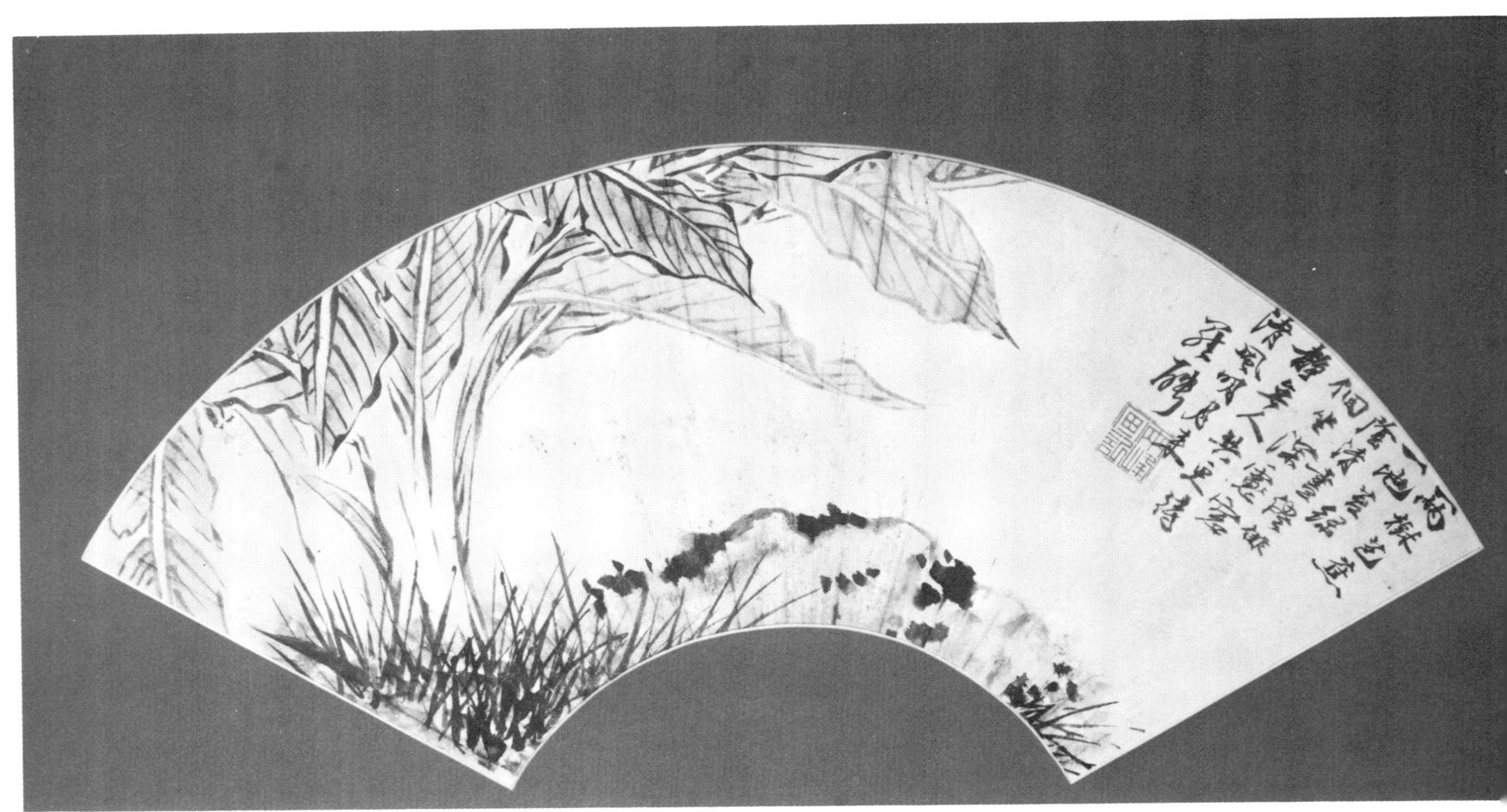

among literati friends. The thick stalks and large, ribbed leaves of two banana trees, positioned at the lower left corner of the arched fan, are balanced at the opposite side by the artist's inscription and seal. In literati painting, the painted image is always complemented and enhanced by poetic inscriptions. Calligraphic inscriptions were seldom emphasized on these paintings created before the thirteenth and fourteenth centuries. Inscriptions reminded the viewer of the two-dimensional surface of the painting and destroyed the realistic illusion that was so evident in the earlier tenth-century monumental landscapes (see Figs. 14, 18). As literati, they were first of all writers and did not attempt to create "true-to-life" images in their paintings. It is therefore understandable that their works reveal a symbiotic relationship between painting and poetry. Lo P'ing's inscription does not describe the banana trees, symbols of scholarly virtue, but shares his moment of artistic inspiration. Although alone, he is not lonely. He finds solace in the banana trees, the rising moon, and the refreshing wind.

> *A pair of banana tress on a moss-covered knoll*
> *On a sunlit day you can stroll beneath their green*
> *   shade.*
> *Sitting in solitude at my window, I share this tranquil*
> *   moment with*
> *Only the fresh breezes and the promise of a bright*
> *   moon.*

Ling-yun Shih Liu, trans.

Fig. 28. *Banana Trees.* Album leaf, ink and color on paper. Lo P'ing, 1733–1799, Ch'ing Dynasty. Anonymous loan.

Calligraphy was considered a high art form by China's intellectual elite many centuries before painting joined the other expressive arts. Although a highly disciplined skill, callligraphy allowed the individual artist freedom for personal interpretation. While contemporary Western viewers unfamiliar with the Chinese language usually regard a calligraphic inscription only as a visual art, it meant far more to the Chinese scholar. First of all, it was a necessary tool or skill of his occupation, for he spent his days writing official documents. Second, and more important, it was the supreme test of the cultivated individual, communicating much more than the written word. Like penmanship in Western cultures that reveals unique and individualistic traits of a person, Chinese calligraphy was a visual and tangible testimony of the personality and virtue of the scholar.

Scholar-amateurs knew that their skill as painters was dependent upon their skill as calligraphers. Certainly the skill in handling brush and ink — essential elements of both calligraphy and painting — learned through long hours of calligraphic practice can be naturally transferred to the art of painting. The added, intangible ingredient of both a masterful painter and calligrapher is, however, talent.

Chao Meng-fu (1254–1322), one of the founding fathers of the literati movement, was even in his own time considered to be among China's most talented calligraphers and painters. A descendant of the imperial family that ruled China during the Sung Dynasty, he retired to his home in Wu-hsing, Chechiang, when the Sung Dynasty was conquered in 1279 by Mongolian invaders. Unlike the majority of scholars who were forced to abandon their government occupations, he was invited in 1286 to the court of Kublai Khan. He later was appointed the enviable position of director

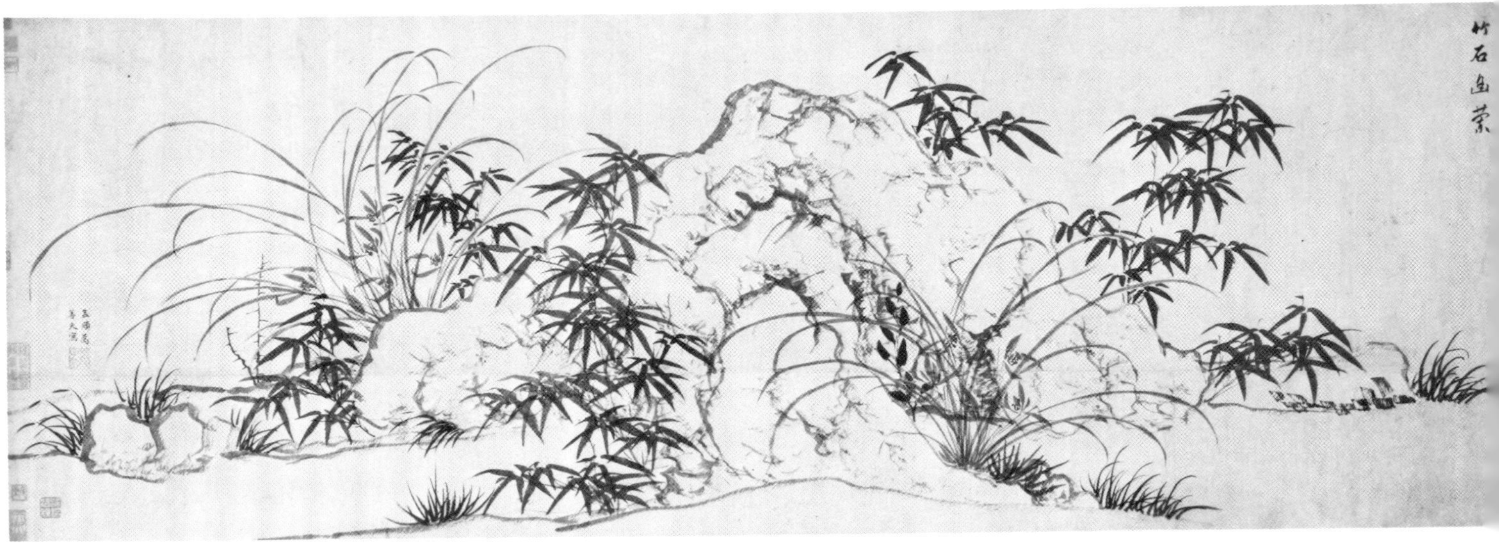

Fig. 29. *Bamboo, Rocks, and Lonely Orchids*. Handscroll, ink on paper. Chao Meng-fu, 1254–1322, Yüan Dynasty. Purchase, John L. Severance Fund. 63.515 [81]

of the Hanlin Academy, an organization whose membership included only the highest ranking literati.

Bamboo, Rocks, and Lonely Orchids (Fig. 29) demonstrates Chao's skill as an experimental artist who was one of the first literati to fully transfer brush techniques generally associated with calligraphy to the related art of painting. In his handscroll, dark wet ink strokes denote the young bamboo plants, the graceful leaves of the orchids, and their clusters of small blossoms. In

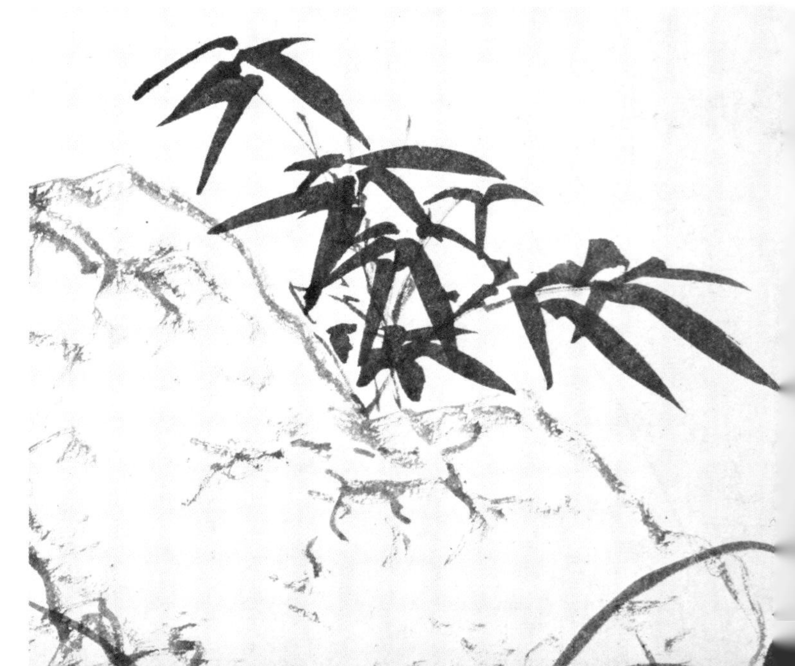

Fig. 30. "Flying-White" Brushstroke (detail) from *Bamboo, Rocks, and Lonely Orchids*.

contrast, the "flying-white," or *fei-pai*, stroke (Fig. 30), made with a drier ink, outlines and contours the rock's surface. Also used by the contemporary scholar-calligrapher Yang Wei-chen (1296–1370) in his inscription on a handscroll in the Freer Gallery of Art in Washington, D.C. (Fig. 31), the stroke is made by applying pressure to the tip of the brush so the hairs separate to expose the white surface of the paper. In Chao's painting (Fig. 30), the brushstroke is distinctive in itself yet still descriptive of the craggy, rough-textured surface of the rock. Chao's ingenious, yet casual use of the meandering stroke gives the impression of "playing" with ink.

The literati selected the themes of their paintings carefully. Landscapes, without doubt, continued to be

Fig. 31. Poem and Colophon to Tsou Fu-lei (detail) from *A Breath of Spring*. Handscroll, ink on paper. Yang Wei-chen, 1296–1370. Courtesy of the Smithsonian Institution, Freer Gallery of Art, Washington, D.C.

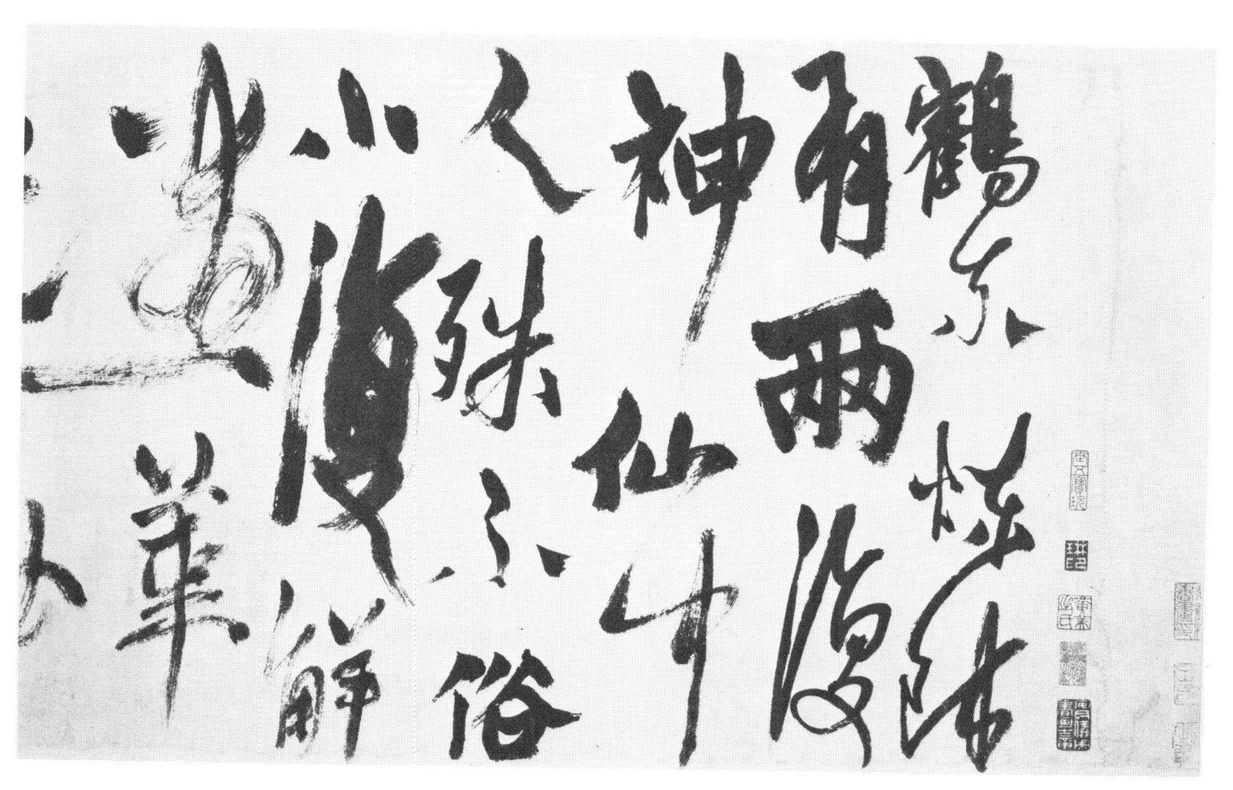

the most popular subject. Figure painting, genre scenes, and brightly colored bird-and-flower themes (decorative subjects preferred by professional painters), however, were seldom represented. Instead, monochromatic paintings of certain botanical subjects were the favored themes that remained the insignias of scholar-amateur painters from the twelfth through the nineteenth centuries. The works of Chao Meng-fu (Fig. 29), Ni Tsan (Fig. 37), Wang Mien (Fig. 33), and Li Shan (Fig. 34) illustrate the cherished themes of pine trees, bamboo, and branches of the flowering plum.

The pine tree emerged as an important theme independent of the landscape setting during the late T'ang Dynasty, while bamboo and plum appeared later in the twelfth century under the influence of the literati. Collectively called the "Three Friends" of Chinese art, these noble plants became so popular in succeeding centuries that they were also frequently used as decorative motifs on textiles, lacquer, and porcelain, where the design was brushed under the glaze in cobalt blue (Fig. 32).

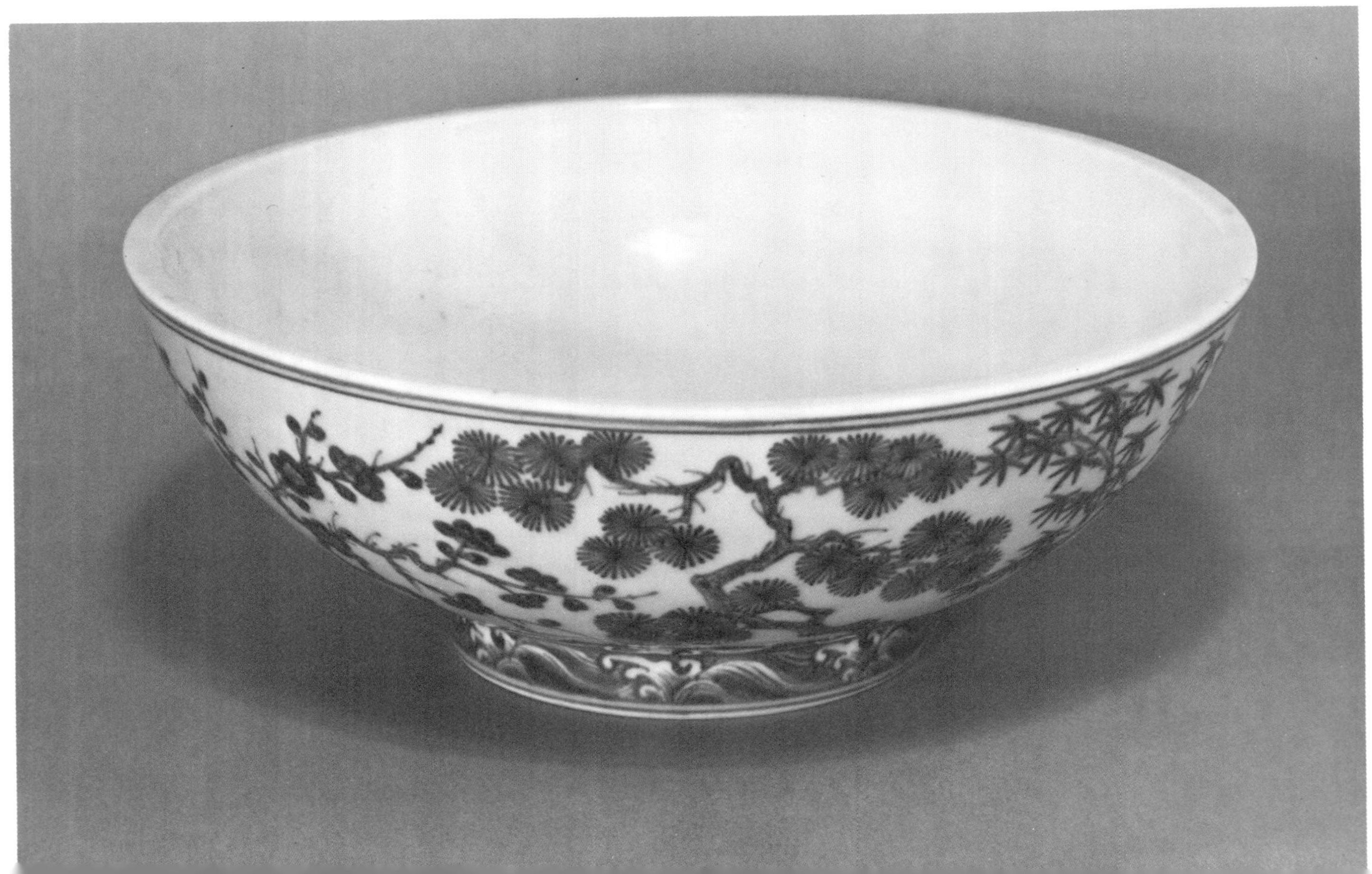

Scholar-amateur artists revered the botanical trinity for its symbolic connotations rather than for its decorative beauties. The tree and plants signified admirable virtues of the scholar-gentleman. The pine tree that remains green throughout the year represents age and endurance. The blossoming plum, which produces no fruit, blooms early in the spring before the snow has melted. It symbolizes strength and rebirth. Twelfth-century poets idolized the plum and supposedly became exhilarated from eating its delicately scented sweet buds. Bamboo, the most beloved of all plants, denotes perseverance and an open mind. Its hollow yet flexible stem bends in the wind and rain but always returns to a vertical position and is similar to the Confucian gentleman who maintains his moral principles despite the trials of daily existence. Bamboo was so intimately associated with the scholar that poets simply called it "that gentleman." Literati painters believed paintings of the "Three Friends" should not be viewed for their literal, painted images but for their symbolic and expressive qualities. Since the brush techniques used in painting bamboo, pine, and plum branches are similar to those required for calligraphy, artists strove to achieve in their paintings of the noble plants the same abstract qualities admired in calligraphy.

Fig. 32. *Dice Bowl with Decoration of the "Three Friends."* Porcelain, underglaze cobalt design. Ming Dynasty, mark and reign of Hsüan-te, 1426–1436. Purchase, John L. Severance Fund. CMA 53.631

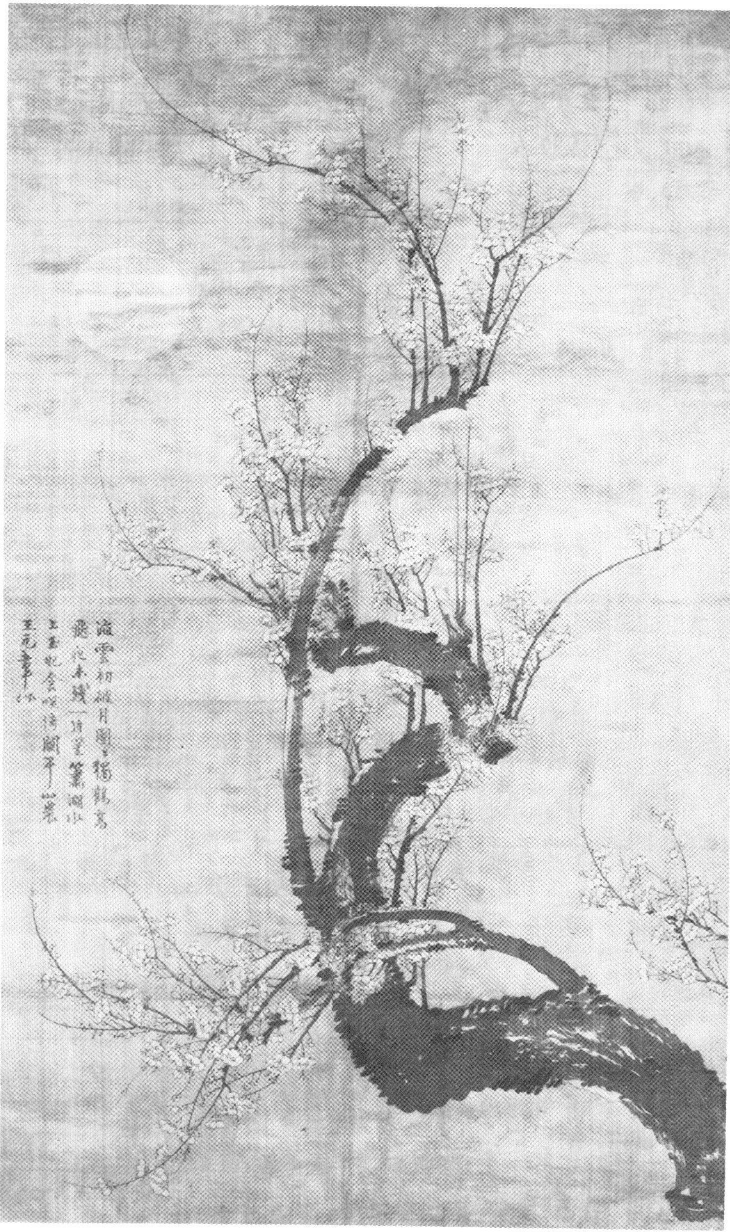

Fig. 33. *A Prunus in the Moonlight.* Hanging scroll, ink on silk. Wang Mien, 1287–1359, Yüan Dynasty. Purchase, Leonard C. Hanna Jr. Bequest. CMA 74.26 [83]

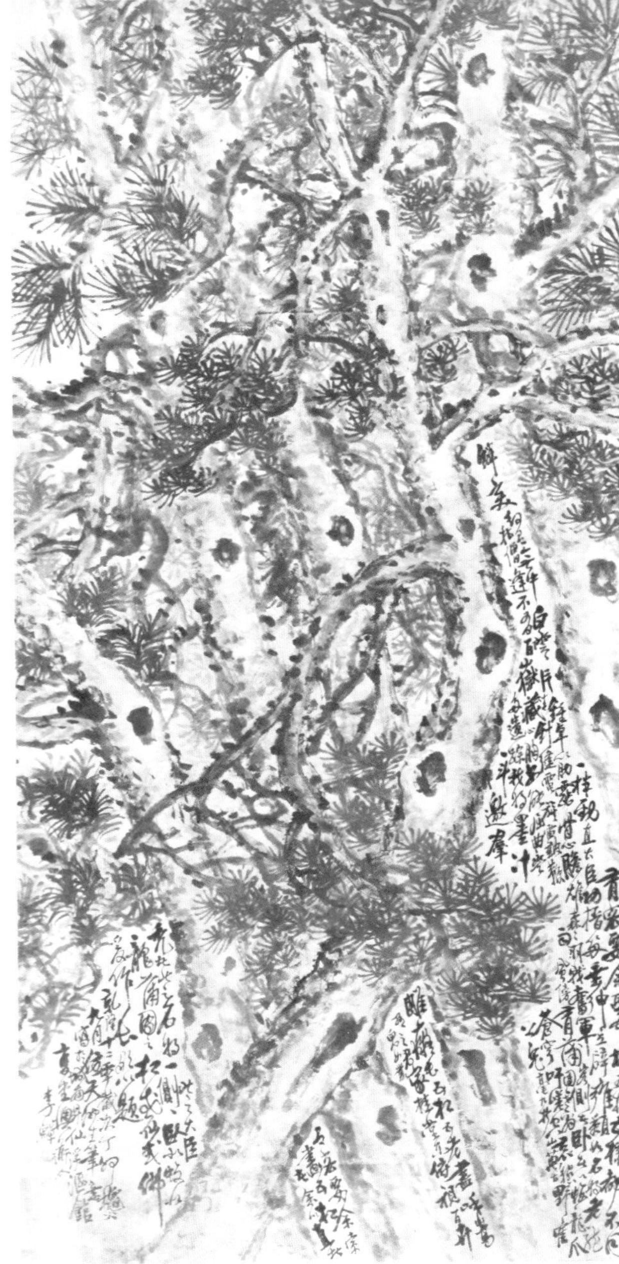

Fig. 34. *Five Pine Trees.* Hanging scroll, ink on paper, dated 1747. Li Shan, ca. 1686–1762, Ch'ing Dynasty. Purchase from the J. H. Wade Fund. CMA 76.112 [268]

Wang Mien (1287–1359) was the most famous painter of blossoming plum branches during the Yüan Dynasty. He planted a thousand plum trees around his home and called it ''The Plum Blossom Retreat.'' An eccentric who always dressed in old clothes and studied the martial arts, he refused to serve in a governmental office and devoted his life to homage of the plum trees through such paintings as *A Prunus in the Moonlight* (Fig. 33).

Graceful branches of the tree wind sinuously across the surface of the large, silk hanging scroll. Wang's masterful brush technique is evident in the bold, energetic ''flying-white'' brushstrokes of the sturdy branch and the elegant, linear strokes that define the brittle twigs. The artist carefully toned the surface of the silk with a pale ink but left untouched the interior of the outlined blossoms and the circular moon. Their delicate hues are simply the natural, unpainted color of the silk. Wang's short poem reinforces the poetic vision of the plum branches in the moonlight. He suggests the regenerative capabilities of the tree and its enduring, pure beauty by the traditional emblems of immortality — a crane and the precious stone, jade. Wang's ''jade-lady'' and constant companion was the plum tree.

A full moon appears at the break of the sea of clouds,
The single crane is flying high before the night is gone.
Above the lake, the air is filled with music of flute
  and panpipe.
And the ''jade lady'' is leaning against the railing
  with a smile.

Wai-kam Ho, trans.

Five Pine Trees (Fig. 34), a hanging scroll painted in the autumn of 1747 by the eccentric scholar-painter Li Shan (ca. 1686–1762), innovatively and dramatically combines both written and painted descriptions of the pine tree. During the reign of the Kang-hsi emperor, Li Shan enjoyed imperial favor but eventually suffered disapproval and, ultimately, dismissal from the court. After 1742 he spent the mature years of his painting career in his birthplace, Yangchou, Chechiang. Five years after his retirement there, he painted the large hanging scroll that is only one of a series of paintings illustrating a favorite theme and poem.

The entire surface of the painting is densely packed with pine trunks, bark, needles, and hastily written, unorganized lines of calligraphy. The inscription identifies the pine trees as portraits of mythological and religious deities and great men.

A friend asked me to paint the five pines.
I associated the straight pine with a statesman,
the bald one with a famous general, the one leaning
to one side with dragons, the short one with foliage
like a grass-mat with either an immortal or Buddha.

Henry Kleinhenz and Ling-yun Shih Liu, trans.

Li Shan was not the first Chinese artist to see in the bark-covered, undulating trunks and branches of the pine the withering, scale-covered body of a dragon. A Taoist and imperial symbol, it is one of the most common motifs in Chinese art. The remaining pines represent either a Buddha or an immortal (referring to the leading religions, Buddhism and Taoism), a general, and a statesman. These men, respected for their age, wisdom, and strength have, like the pine, remained enduring symbols of Chinese society. Li created through mere brush and ink a complex unity of calligraphy and pictorial imagery.

Pine, bamboo, and flowering plum branches were also known as the "Three Friends of the Wintry Season" because they thrive during the cold winter months. This botanical trilogy took on special connotations during the thirteenth and fourteenth centuries. It became synonymous with the scholar-recluses or scholars-in-retirement who lived as a subculture of society below the Yangtze River.

Reclusion or voluntary withdrawal from society and civic duties was not unusual for the Confucian scholar-official. In politically corrupt times it was a respected and legitimate form of political protest for the official who could not maintain his personal integrity in his public office. At these times, early retirement was not only an acceptable alternative but an admirable, virtuous one. Even in peaceful times, however, the desire to escape from wearisome, bureaucratic routine to the solitude of nature or the companionship of friends was as inherent to the Confucian scholar as his moral responsibility to serve his nation. Literary inscriptions by these scholars refer to the world of politics and the pettiness of daily existence as "the dusty world."

The "Peach Blossom Spring" (Fig. 35), a literary theme represented in a small album leaf attributed to Shih Jui (active ca. 1426–ca. 1470), illustrates the utopian existence desired by the scholar-officials. The model for all scholar-recluses, Tao Yüan-ming (365–427) retired from official life at age thirty-three to raise chrysanthemums and write poetry and prose. His "Peach Blossom Spring" recounts the experiences of a lost fisherman whose boat came to a grove of peach trees in full bloom. Beyond the grove, a secret opening in the hillside led him to a secluded prosperous village, where he was welcomed with food and drink and stories of village ancestors who fled to this refuge during the turbulent years of the Ch'in Dynasty (221–206 BC). Cut

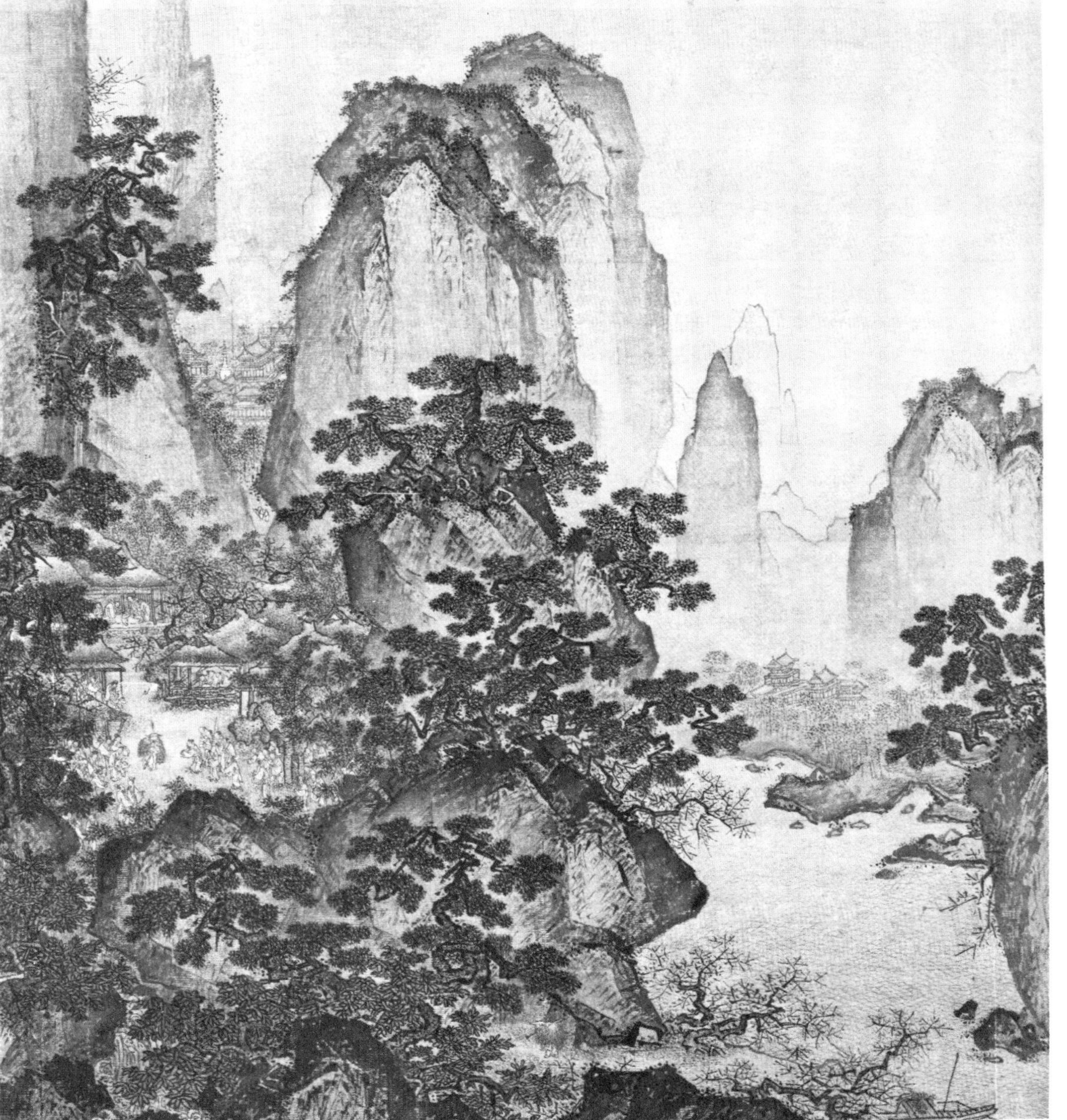

off from the entire world for hundreds of years, the small village was happily unaware of either past or present history. The inhabitants requested that the fisherman tell no one of their existence. Although he was careful to mark his path when he left, the fisherman never again found the hidden world of the "Peach Blossom Spring."

The "Peach Blossom Spring" was a popular subject among both literati and professional painters. In his album leaf *The Haven of the Peach-Blossom Spring* (Fig. 35), Shih Jui, a fifteenth-century court painter working during the early Ming Dynasty, depicted the fisherman's arrival at the world of Shangri-la. His boat is anchored under the peach trees. A circle of villagers greet the fisherman who is dressed in the customary straw raincoat. Shih Jui created the impression of an isolated world through a barrier of crystalline rocks and erratically shaped trees that separate the outside "civilized" world from the secluded hamlet. The precise, meticulous brushwork that dominates the small painting is characteristic of this artist who gave equal emphasis to landscape elements and narrative theme.

For the majority of scholars living during the thirteenth and fourteenth centuries around the cities of Hangchou and Suchou, seclusion was an involuntary alternative forced upon them by the aggressive, nomadic Mongols who overthrew the Chinese Southern Sung Dynasty at the end of the thirteenth century. During the following eighty-nine years of the Yüan Dynasty, the scholarly class was unable to pursue its

occupation or goals. At the beginning of this era, the Mongol emperors abolished the civil service examination, the scholars' only avenue for social and occupational success. Although a select number of scholars were invited to serve at the Yüan court, only a few, such as Chao Meng-fu, accepted. The scholar-officials who served under the previous Southern Sung Dynasty declined the invitation because they strongly felt it was morally wrong to ally themselves with a foreign power. Like the "Three Friends of the Wintry Season" that could withstand the cold, these men maintained their scholarly integrity even during the harsh years of Mongolian rule. They viewed the previous Sung Dynasty as their "Peach Blossom Spring."

Bitter and resentful, the literati sought only the sympathetic companionship of close friends. In their poetry they nostalgically referred to the past. In their painting, now a type of political aesthetic protest, they recalled the older styles associated with native Chinese dynasties. As scholar-officials, they formed a closed society, a subculture that privately nurtured their ideals and provided sympathy for their position in history.

Wu Chen (Fig. 36 and Cover) and Ni Tsan (Fig. 37), two of the greatest scholar-amateur painters of the Yüan Dynasty, epitomize the literati tradition in their lives and works. Aloof and reserved, both artists became true recluses during their painting careers and were fortunate enough to escape the rebellions during the middle of the fourteenth century in the Chiangnan region where they lived. Their works are timeless examples of the literati taste for simple, unassertive images.

Wu Chen (1280–1354), the older of the two painters, made his living as a fortuneteller, one of the lowly occupations chosen by scholars during the Yüan Dynasty because of their study of the classical text, the *Book of Changes (I-ching)*. Later, Wu Chen retired completely

Fig. 35. *The Haven of the Peach-Blossom Spring*. Album leaf, ink and color on silk. Shih Jui (attributed to), active ca. 1426–ca. 1470, Ming Dynasty. Purchase from the John L. Severance Fund. CMA 52.283 [137]

from society and only exchanged his paintings for food and other necessities. Like Wang Mien, he planted plum trees around his home and named himself the Plum Blossom Taoist. *Poetic Feeling in a Thatched Pavilion* (Fig. 36 and Cover), a handscroll painted in 1347 by Wu Chen only seven years before his death, demonstrates the artist's personal style as well as his desire for the private existence of a recluse.

The enjoyment of any literati painting is not solely dependent upon the visual experience. The inscriptions provide a deeper understanding of the artist's feelings and are as important as the painted image. Wu Chen's inscription at the end, or left side, of the scroll enhances the quiet scene of two friends visiting in the small, open pavilion.

By the side of the hamlet I built a thatched pavilion. Balanced and squared, it is lofty in conception. The woods being deep, birds are happy; the dust being distant, bamboos and pines are clean. Streams and rocks invite lingering enjoyment, lutes and books please my temperament. How should I bid farewell to the world of the ordinary and the familiar, and let my heart go its own way for the gratification of my life?

Wai-kam Ho, trans.

Fig. 36. *Poetic Feeling in a Thatched Pavilion*. Handscroll, ink on paper, dated 1347. Wu Chen, 1280–1354, Yüan Dynasty. Purchase, Leonard C. Hanna Jr. Bequest. CMA 63.259 [109]

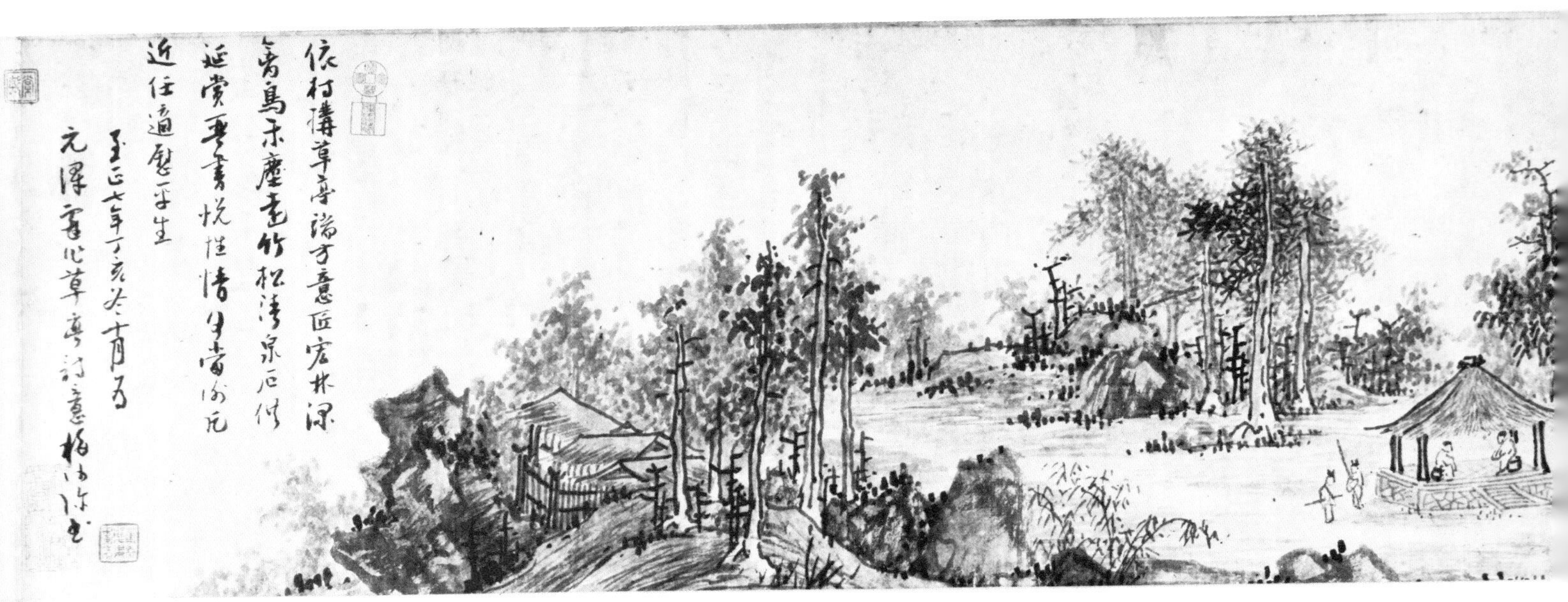

Fig. 37. *Bamboo, Rock, and Tall Tree*. Hanging scroll, ink on paper. Ni Tsan, 1301–1374, Yüan Dynasty. Purchase, Leonard C. Hanna Jr. Bequest. CMA 78.65 [110]

Wu Chen's detachment from society is evident in the phrase "the dust being distant, bamboos and pines are clean." Because the "dusty world" is far away, the bamboos and pines — or, according to traditional symbolism, the hermit-scholars — are clean. Withdrawn from the political arena, the literati could remain spiritually pure.

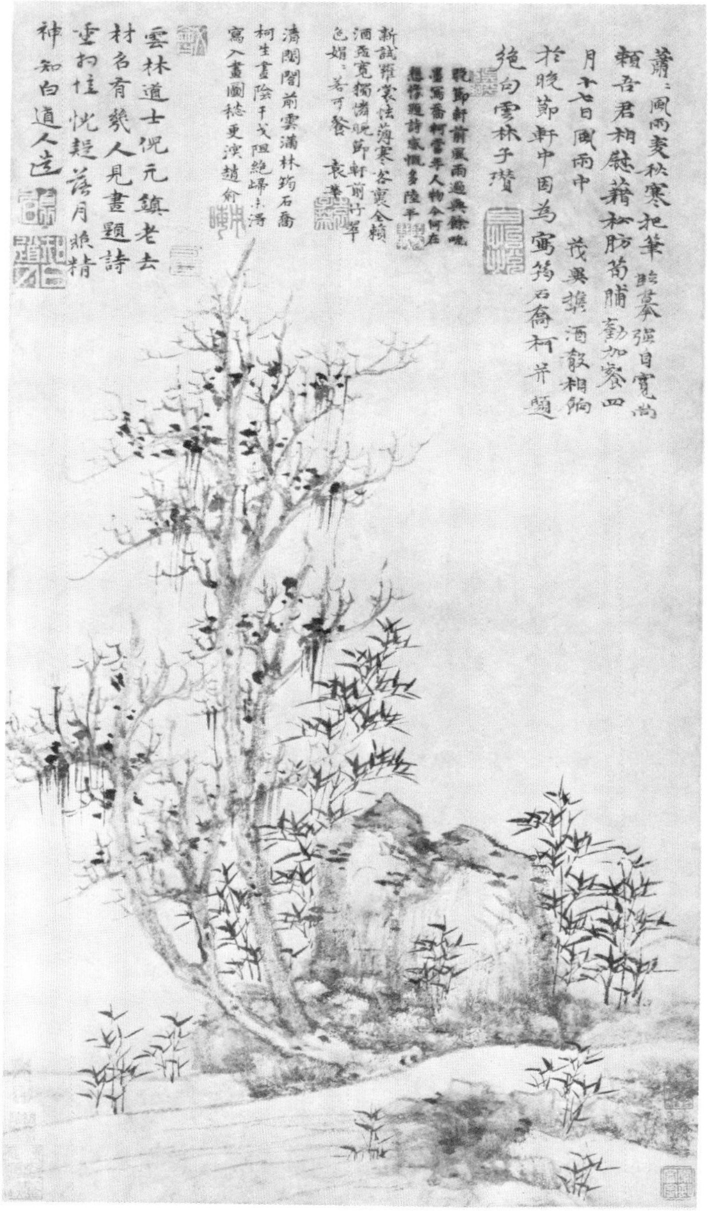

Wu Chen's brushwork is as "balanced and squared" as his small thatched hut (Cover). In contrast to Chao Meng-fu's "flying-white" stroke (Fig. 30) or Li Sung's

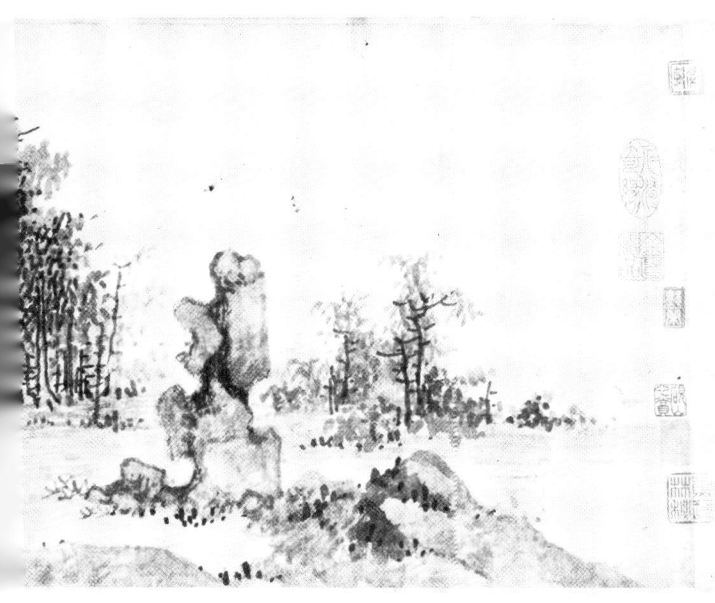

thin, sharp strokes (see Fig. 7), Wu Chen's brushstrokes are thick and blunt. They are created "by keeping a relatively even pressure on the brush, which is held vertically, its tip remaining always within the stroke. . . ."[11] His steady, controlled brushwork is called the "single-stroke" style and was developed from the flexible brush techniques of Chü-jan.

Ni Tsan (1301–1374), an eccentric who was obsessed with cleanliness, used his family inheritance to build a noteworthy collection of paintings and calligraphy and a large library. Like so many other wealthy landowners living in the Chiangnan region who suffered heavy taxation under the Mongolian government, Ni Tsan was forced to divide his property among family and friends. He renounced the corrupt and inhospitable society completely sometime after 1345 and spent the rest of his life traveling in a houseboat throughout the Lake T'ai area. He occasionally visited Buddhist monasteries or the homes of close friends. His paintings, recognized as the work of an artistic genius, were in great demand during his lifetime.

The timeworn adage "You can see the man in his work" may sound trite by contemporary standards. Nonetheless, Ni Tsan's paintings, such as *Bamboo, Rock, and Tall Tree* (Fig. 37), are perfect examples of the genuineness and truthfulness the statement held for the literati. Ni's work, devoid of human presence, reflects the cool, wintry temperament of this scholar-recluse.

Ni achieved an air of chilliness in his painting partly through his sparing use of ink, a characteristic of his style. It was said that Ni treasured ink "as if it were gold." The dryness of his brush and distinctive style is evident in his use of the "flying-white" stroke that creates the rocks, symbols of the scholar's steadfast nature (Fig. 38). Chao Meng-fu originally combined the "flying-white" stroke with the rock motif in his hand-scroll *Bamboo, Rocks, and Lonely Orchids* (Fig. 29), using the brushstroke in such a way that the viewer is conscious of his casual and undulating gesture. In contrast, Ni Tsan used the stroke to create a transparent image so that the viewer remains unaware of the artist's presence. His paintings exemplify the literati ideal of, and desire for, blandness and purity in their works.

The somber ambience of *Bamboo, Rock, and Tall Tree* is reinforced by the artist's inscription at the upper right of the hanging scroll. His depression during the wintry, rainy day is relieved only by work and the gifts of a close friend. The loneliness expressed in his painting was understood by the literati, and fulfilled their desire for moments of stillness that allowed them the time to replenish their spiritual natures and to escape from the "dusty world."

> *Windy and rainy days — what a chilly wheat-harvesting season,*
> *With brush in hand, I fight depression by copying.*
> *Fortunately, I can depend upon you, my friend, to send me consolation —*
> *"Pine-lard" wine, and meat with bamboo shoots that never fail to awaken the appetite.*

Wai-kam Ho, trans.

In their own time the literati were intellectually, socially, and artistically far above and far removed from their world. They revolutionized Chinese painting by changing the standards of artistic creation. As an act of creation, painting was for them an aesthetic and mental escape from the world. As visual enjoyment, painting enabled them to transcend the "dusty" world.

Fig. 38. *Bamboo, Rock, and Tall Tree* (detail).

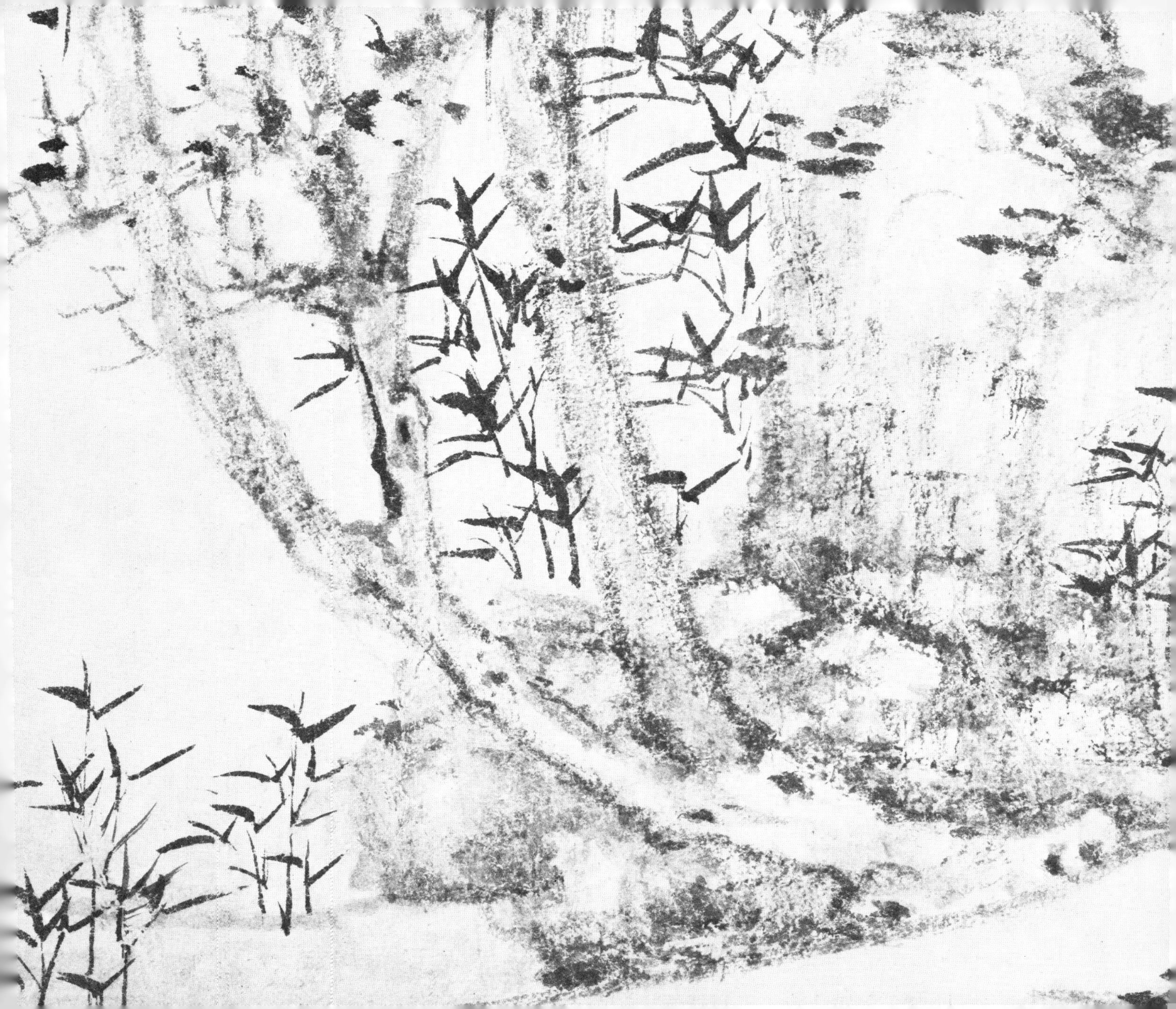

Accessories of the Scholar's Studio

The scholar's studio was his own world, within, yet still apart from the outside "dusty" world. As the literati painters rose to a position of prominence during the fourteenth century, their studios often appeared in their works. The studio, the master's private quarters in his home, also served as a library or study and fulfilled the needs of both a scholar and an artist. As a sphere of artistic and intellectual creativity, it housed the scholar's personal collection of paintings and antiquities as well as the treasured books and old manuscripts necessary for the pursuit of wisdom. Only the closest of friends were invited into this lofty sanctum. The room silently communicated the most intimate characteristics about the man, and everything within it from the simplest of brushes, ink sticks, and inkstones to the non-functional, oddly shaped rocks or pieces of wood expressed his personality. The studio was the artist's private, aesthetic world.

Literary sources and many literati paintings reveal one architectural feature essential in any artist's studio —a window. In his treatise *An Essay on Landscape Painting (Lin Ch'üan Kao Chih)*, Kuo Hsi included a window in the description of the special rituals that his father observed in preparing himself to paint: "he would seat himself before a bright window, put his desk in order, and burn incense right and left."[12] While the smoking incense sanctified his creative space, the bright window satisfied an elemental, essential requirement for either painting or studying, serving as the major source of light for an interior lit only by oil lamps.[13] Equally significant, however, the window extended the artist's working space into the nearby, familiar landscape. An artist, such as Lo P'ing who probably painted the *Banana Trees* (see Fig. 28) while seated before his studio window, studied nature's forms without ever leaving the comfortable confines of his home. A lone figure seated literally at the window in a painting or figuratively in a poetic inscription implied the artist's physical presence, or absence, from his microcosm. Making use of this imagery in his inscription on Chao Meng-fu's handscroll, *Hsieh Yu-yü in His Mind Landscape*, Ni Tsan alluded to Chao's move north in 1286 to serve at the Mongolian court: "At the 'Gull-Wave Pavilion,' as the moon was fading away, the windows that opened to the night were empty."[14]

The literati painter usually honored his studio with a literary title that was significant only to him, or with another name derived from one of his many pseudonyms. Every Chinese artist proudly claims a number of "fancy names," or *hao*, nicknames he himself selects or that admiring friends bestow upon him. While Chao Meng-fu christened his studio the "Gull-Wave Pavilion," another well-known literati, Wu Chen, named his studio "The Plum Blossom Retreat" in keeping with his pseudonym "The Plum Blossom Taoist."

The studio name was generally inscribed on the flat surface of a seal (Fig. 39). Artists and poets possessed many seals, including a separate one for the studio's title and one for each *hao*. Although seal carving was a proud skill usually associated with craftsmen or professional artisans, most literati designed and carved their own seals. These scholarly painters chose relatively soft materials—horn, ivory, wood. or amber—rather than the extremely hard stone—jade—that required the tools of professional carvers. Since the characters of their names were chipped out of the stone with a knife, seal carving was referred to as "the art of the iron brush."

Generally crowned with mythical animals, perhaps crouching dragons or, in this case (Fig. 39), a reclining unicorn *(ch'i-lin)*, the seals suggest miniature menageries. The functional part and the only reason for the seal's existence is the flat surface, or base, carved with characters in low relief. Inked with a vermilion paste—a mixture of cinnabar, castor oil, and sesame oil—it is pressed against the painting's surface. The red squares or oval circles, easily discernable on the paintings, denote the artist's personal seals, those of his friends, or even those of a collector. The artist Chao Meng-fu inscribed his handscroll *Bamboc, Rocks, and Lonely Orchids* (see Fig. 29) at the lower left side: "Meng-fu drew this for Shan-fu" and stamped it with three different, personal seals. Hsiang Yüan-pien (1525–1590), a connoisseur of paintings and porcelains, affixed his prominent seal on an ivory wrist rest (Fig. 48) that was once in his private collection. Seals not only assist in determining the authenticity of a work, but they also recount the painting's history. For instance, many paintings in the collection of The Cleveland Museum of Art belonged to the connoisseur-collector Liang Ch'ing-

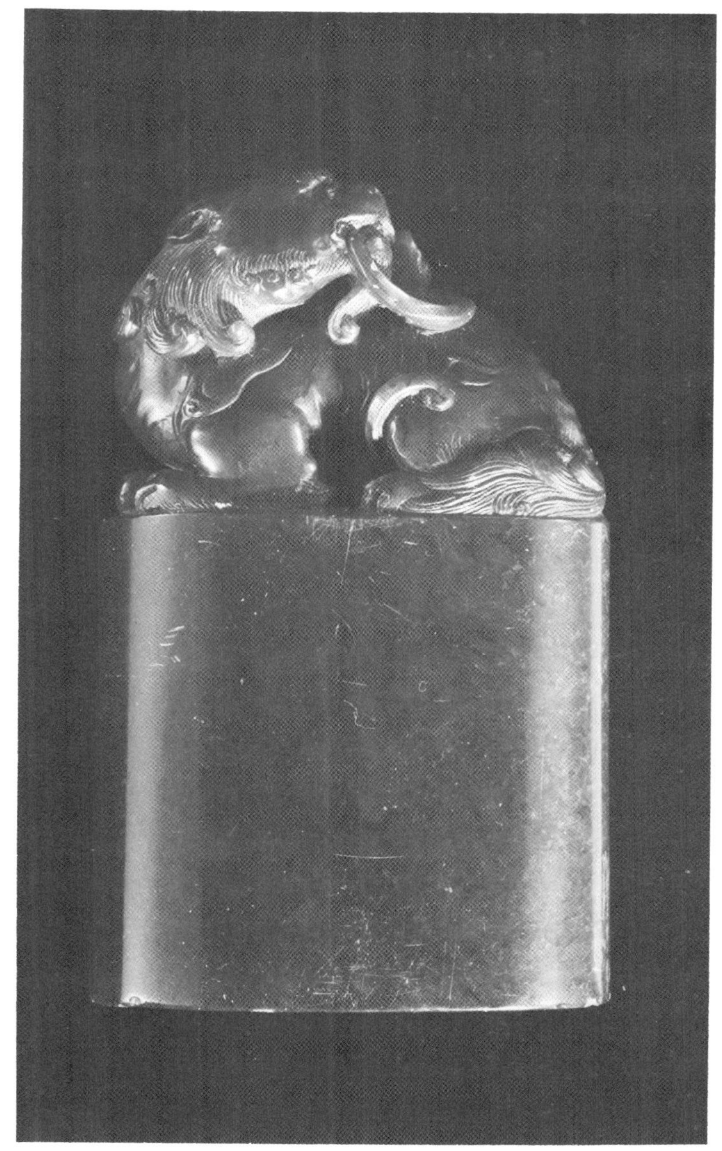

Fig. 39. *Seal with Reclining Ch'i-lin.* Jade. Ch'ing Dynasty, reign of Ch'ien-lung, 1736–1796. Anonymous gift. CMA 52.494

piao (1620–1691). The handscroll by Chao Meng-fu (see Fig. 29) bears sixteen seals of this collector, while Ni Tsan's hanging scroll *Bamboo, Rock, and Tall Tree* (see Fig. 37) has been stamped with only one of Liang Ch'ing-piao's seals.

Brush (Fig. 47), ink (Fig. 43), paper, and the inkstone (Fig. 40) are collectively called the "Four Treasures of the Artist's Studio." In Ch'iu Ying's handscroll *Chao Meng-fu Writing the "Heart" Sutra in Exchange for Tea* (Fig. 41), Chao, with brush in hand, pauses to select the leaves for brewing his tea before beginning to write. The other three treasures rest on the table in front of him. While brush, ink, and paper are soon depleted or worn by constant use, the durable inkstone, the scholar's cherished possession, lasts for centuries.

The inkstone's simple design consists of two parts. The shallow, concave end forms a reservoir for the water, while the smooth, flat surface, when dampened with water from the "well," facilitates the grinding of the inkstone, or cake. With the passing of centuries, the earlier rectangular inkstones—their sides often dis-

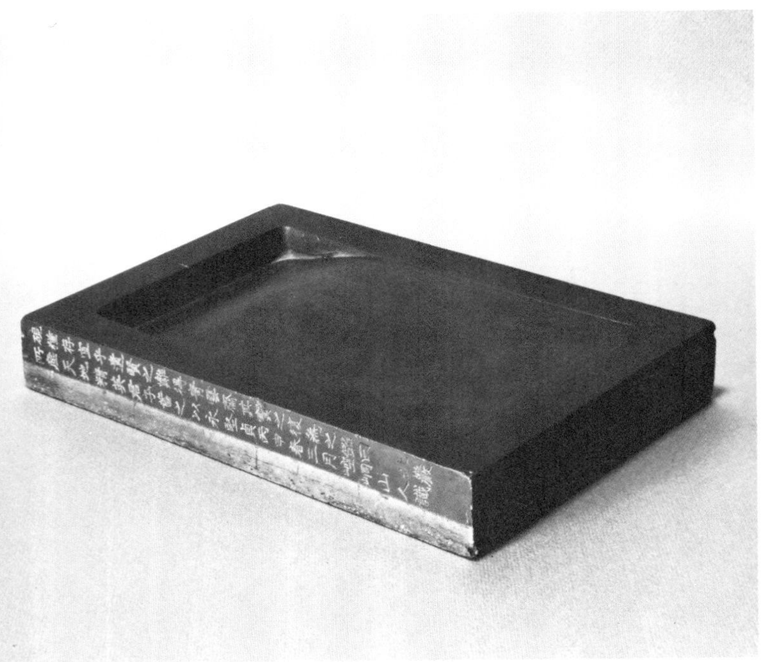

Fig. 40. *Inkstone.* Yüan Dynasty, 1279–1368. Collection of Mr. and Mrs. Wai-kam Ho.

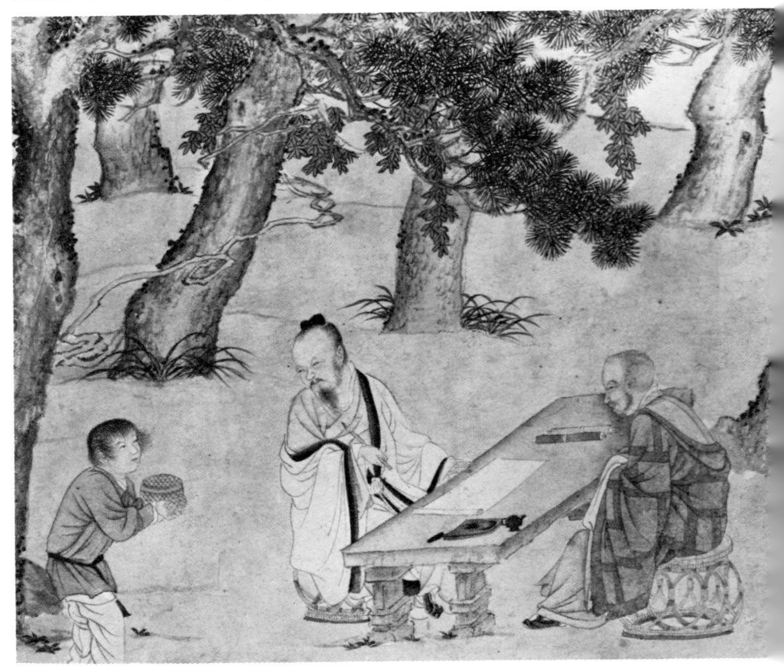

Fig. 41. *Chao Meng-fu Writing the "Heart" Sutra in Exchange for Tea* (detail). Handscroll, ink and color on paper. Ch'iu Ying, 1494/5–1552, Ming Dynasty. Purchase, John L. Severance Fund. CMA 63.102 [165]

creetly inscribed with a favorite poem—were altered, becoming more elaborate in shape and acquiring florid ornamentation. Although traditional, rectangular stones continued to be made, oval inkstones carved with floral or other naturalistic motifs increased in popularity during the Ming and Ch'ing dynasties. It is the inkstone itself that actually determined the ink's quality and, like porcelain, its value can partially be evaluated by sound: a fine inkstone emits a pleasant ring when tapped.

Created out of dense stone taken from quiet waters, an inkstone sustains this relationship with water throughout its lifetime. The best inkstones are from Tuan-hsi, a river located in the southern coastal Kuangtung Province. Distinguished by seven rocky peaks projecting above its surface, the site was discovered during the T'ang Dynasty and called the "Seven Star" cliffs. Stone mined from its first cliff, or grotto, produced such superb inkstones that during the tenth century they were sent as tribute to the imperial court. By the following century, avid collectors had exhausted the supply of this prized stone.

The miniature companions that encircled the artist in his studio frequently reiterated certain popular themes used by Chinese painters. P'u Chung-ch'ien, a seventeenth-century bamboo carver working in Nanking, adapted the common subject of a wise sage seated under a pine tree to the bamboo clip he designed for holding paper (Fig. 42). Similarly, the round ink cake decorated on both sides with molded designs of "one hundred children" (Fig. 43), and the water dropper, only two inches high and modeled in the shape of a boy riding a buffalo (Fig. 45), recall themes illustrated in Southern Sung album leaves (Figs. 44, 46).

Decorative ink cakes served as ornamental gifts for friends even though these were functional objects

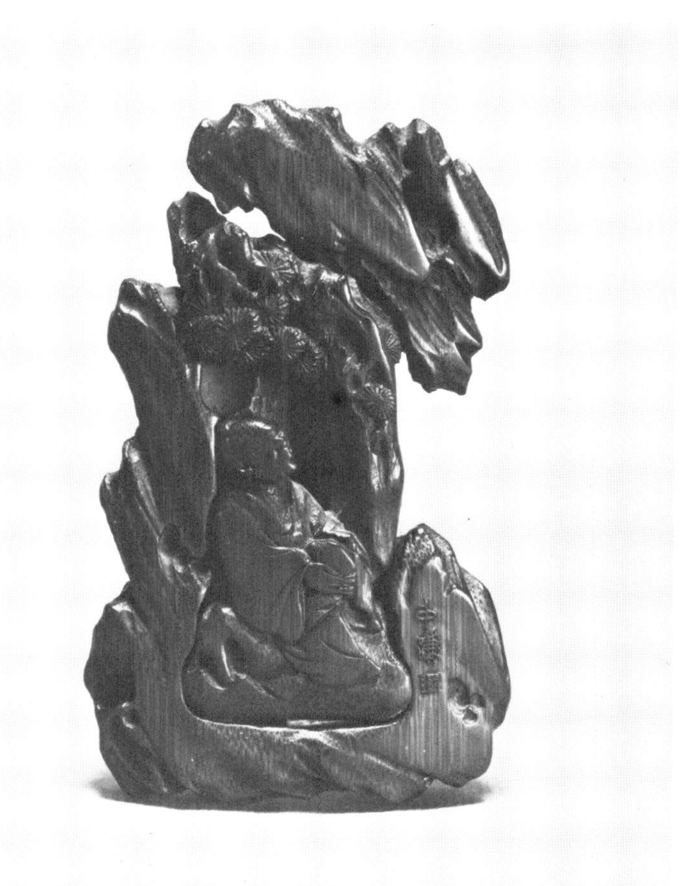

Fig. 42. *Clip for Paper with Sage Seated Under a Pine*. Bamboo. P'u Chung-ch'ien, Ming Dynasty, 17th century. Purchase, Edward L. Whittemore Fund. CMA 77.8

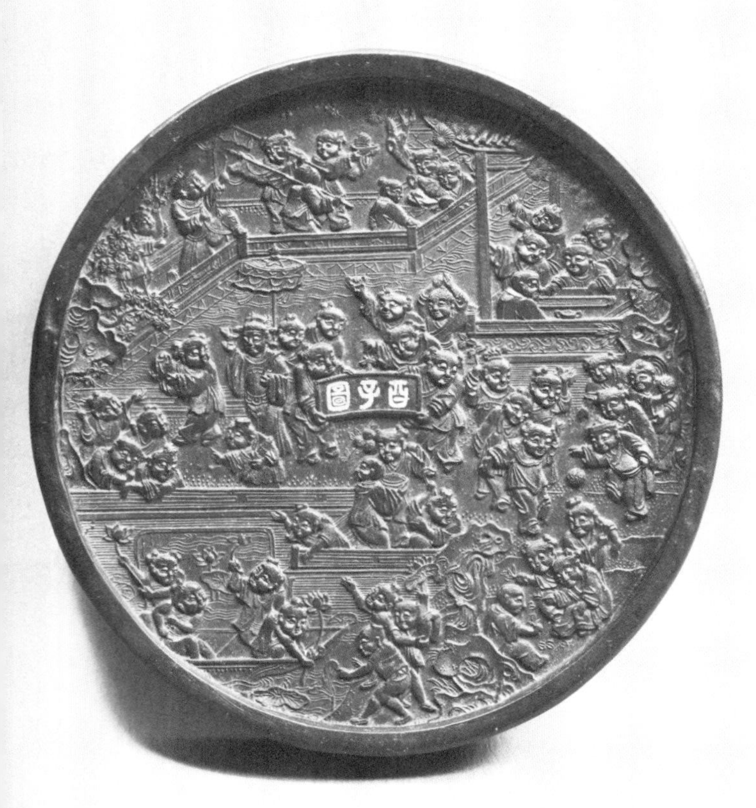

Fig. 43. *Ink Cake with Design of One Hundred Children.* Pine soot, gum. Ming Dynasty, 1368–1644. Gift of Henry W. Kent. CMA 42.214

ening, the cake was often hand painted and inscriptions further embellished with gold. The three incised, gilt characters denoting the "One Hundred Children Picture" *(Pai-tzu t'u)* are centered on a round ink cake (Fig. 43) and identify a theme that was a popular decorative motif during the Ming Dynasty.

One Hundred Children at Play (Fig. 44), a small album leaf painted with ink and color on silk, also illustrates the same theme, but as it was used during the Sung Dynasty. At this earlier date, the "one hundred children" pictures were associated with the joyous festivities held at thirty days, one hundred days, and one year after the birth of a child. Small paintings such as this one made appropriate presents for these birthday celebrations. In both the album painting and the ink cake, youths frolic near a lotus pond. The impersonation of dignitaries, shown here attended by umbrella-carrying servants, appears to have been a favorite game for "one hundred children" either during the Sung or the Yüan Dynasty.

Buffalo and Boy (Fig. 45), which once adorned a scholar's desk, represents the climactic stage in the development of the high-fired, translucent Ch'ing-pai porcelains. Originating during the ninth and tenth centuries and manufactured primarily in the southeastern province of Chianghsi, this type of porcelain is identified by the faint bluish tint of the transparent glaze.

intended also for painting or calligraphy. The manufacture of ink cakes flourished during the Ming Dynasty when they were richly decorated with such designs as dragons, immortals, as well as the conventional symbols of the literati. Ink paste, a mixture of soot and gum (or glue), was pressed into wooden molds carved with decorative designs and inscriptions. After hard-

Fig. 44. *One Hundred Children at Play.* Album leaf, ink and color on silk. Artist unknown, Southern Sung Dynasty, 1127–1279. Purchase from the J. H. Wade Fund. CMA 61.261 [39]

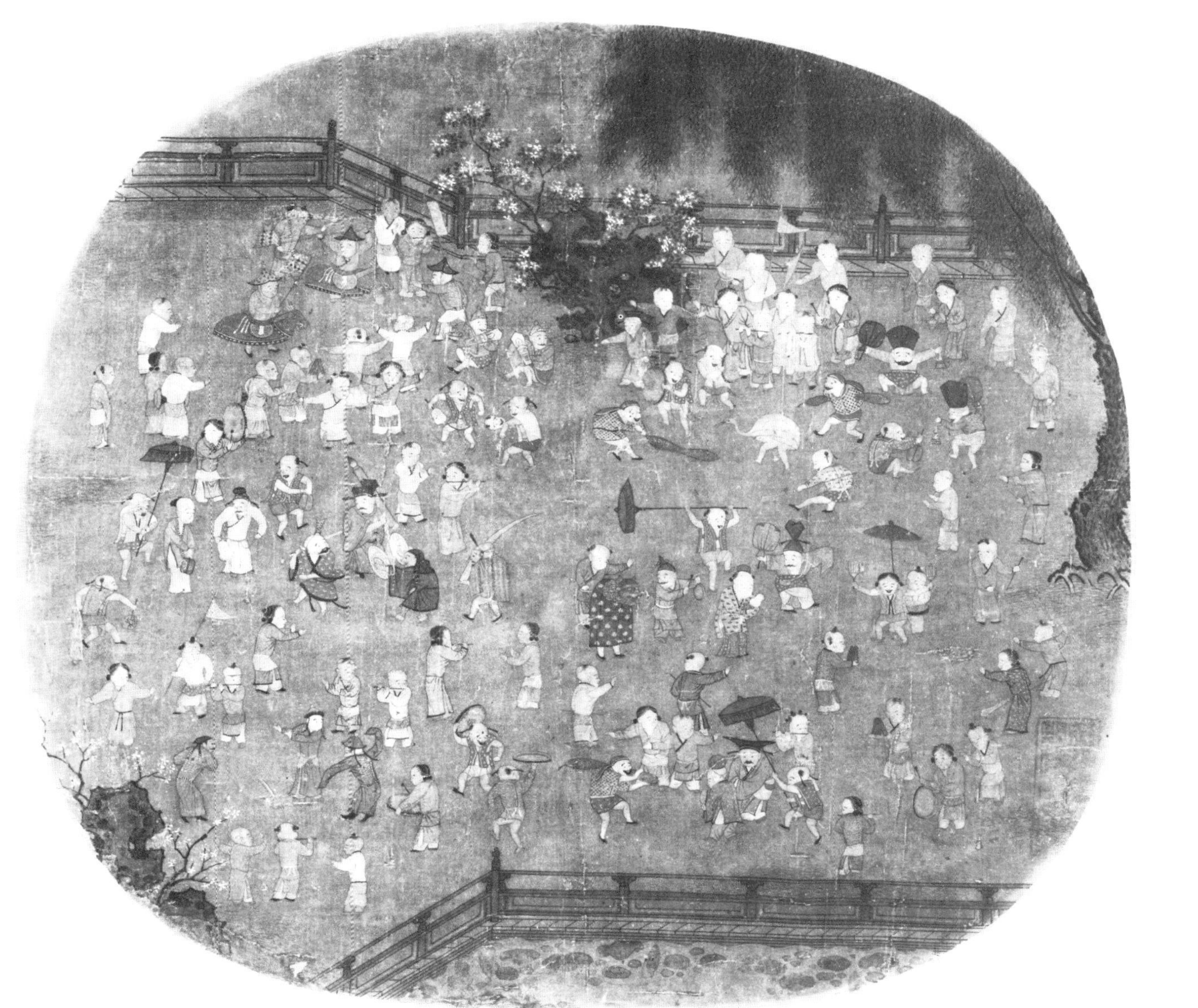

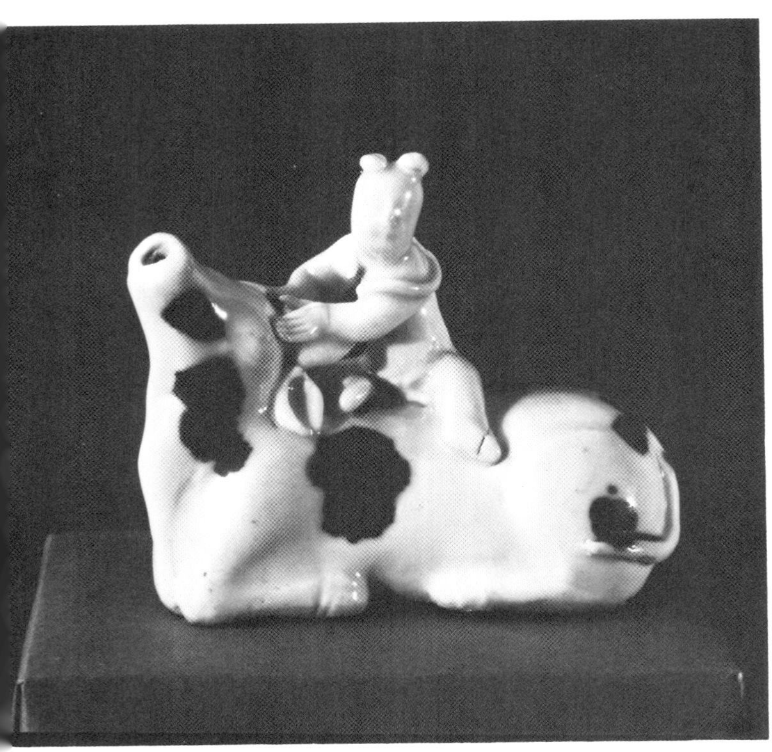

ted the tiny vessel with iron oxide, which turned brown when fired in an oxygen-rich (oxidation) kiln.

In the album leaf *Buffalo Boy* (Fig. 46), Yen Tz'u-p'ing (active ca. 1164–1181) meticulously painted a romantic theme that may be interpreted as either a secular or religious symbol. In the visual language of the literati, the buffalo and boy represented the pleasures of an idyllic, rustic life unencumbered by the "dusty world." According to the teachings of Ch'an (Zen) Buddhism, the bucolic animal also symbolized the earthly part of man's nature.

Although the accessories of the artist's studio reflect that individual's aesthetic values, they are—as finely crafted objects—representative of the collective taste of the era in which they were created. Varying in design and ornamentation, the decorative arts of each dynastic era are generalized statements of that period's prevailing tendencies. The brush (Fig. 47) and ivory wrist rest (Fig. 48), for example, exhibit the preference for intricately carved, naturalistic motifs shared by artisans working during the Ming Dynasty. The bamboo handle of the brush, inscribed with the characters "Made in the Reign of Wan-li of the Great Ming" is intricately patterned with carved, low-relief designs of birds, branches, flowers, and leaves. Approximately nine inches long, the brush was probably a writing tool used in the court of the Wan-li emperor (1573–1619). The

It continued to be produced until the fourteenth and fifteenth centuries, the date of this water dropper, and a period when experimental potters produced innovative shapes and ornamentation.

The reclining buffalo that serves as a pillow for the seated boy is characteristic of these later wares whose shapes were an integral, functional part of the vessels. Water poured from the hollow container passes through the buffalo's open mouth and creates lighter tones when added to dark, black ink. Brown spots, also a characteristic of these fourteenth-century wares, enliven the surface of the water dropper. The potter spot-

Fig. 46. *Buffalo Boy.* Album leaf, ink and color on silk. Yen Tz'u-p'ing, active ca. 1164–1181, Southern Sung Dynasty. Mr. and Mrs. A. Dean Perry Collection.

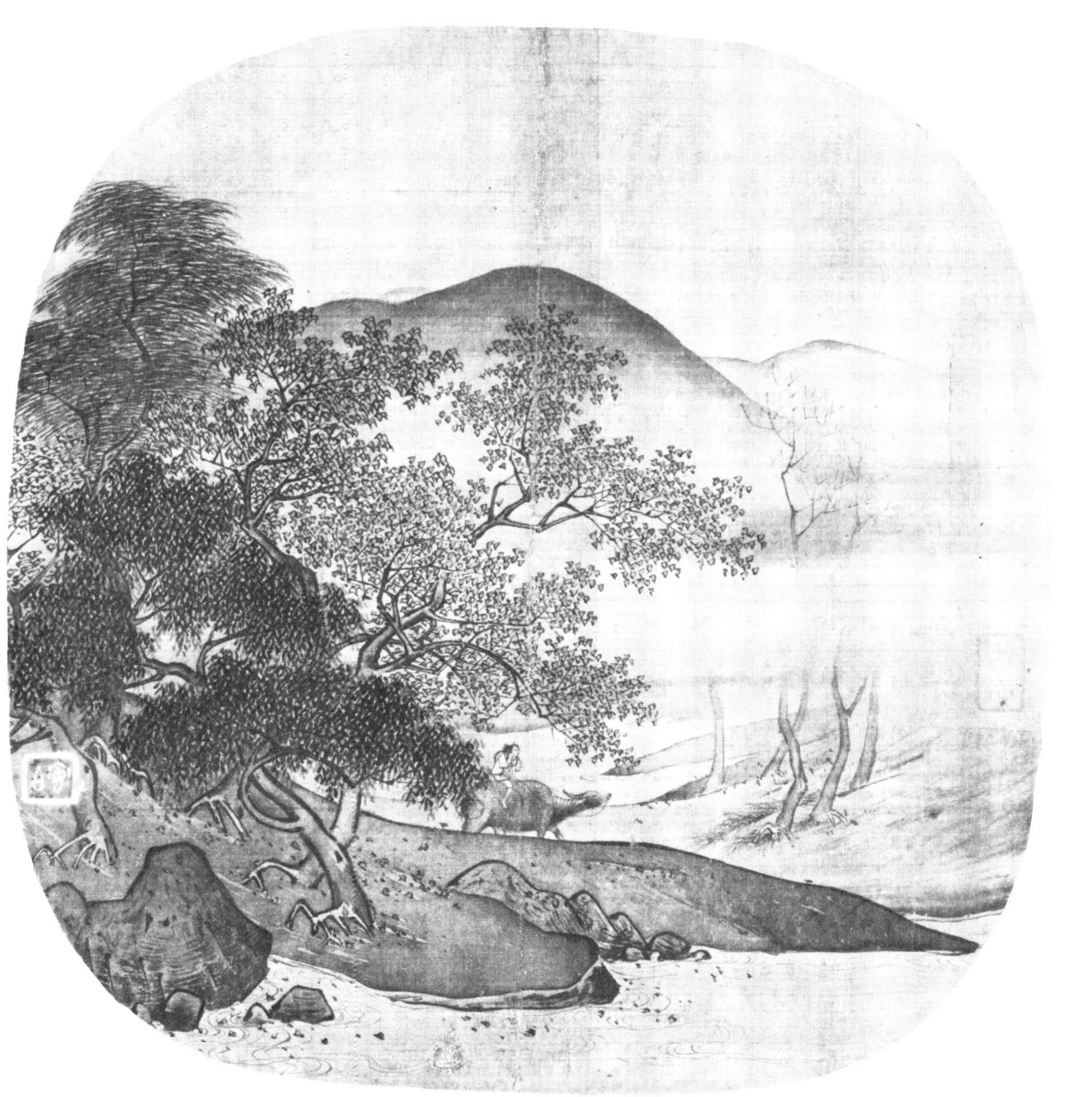

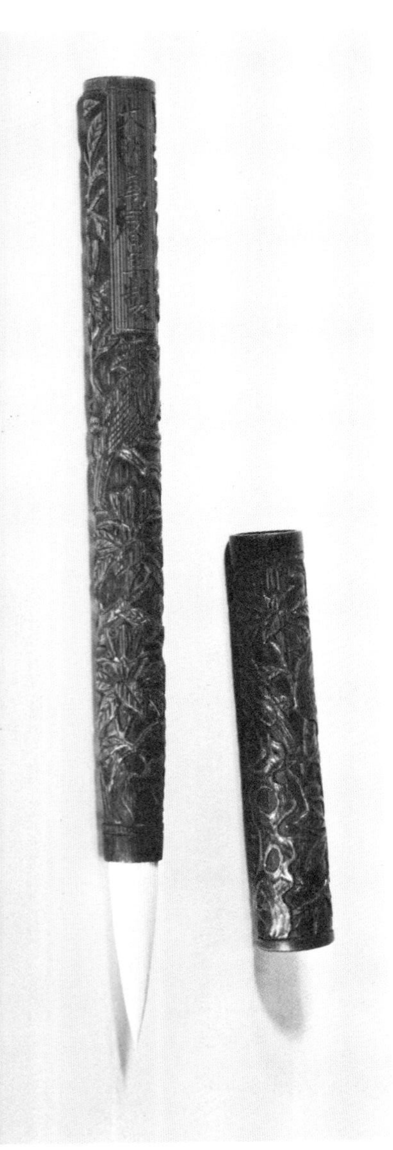
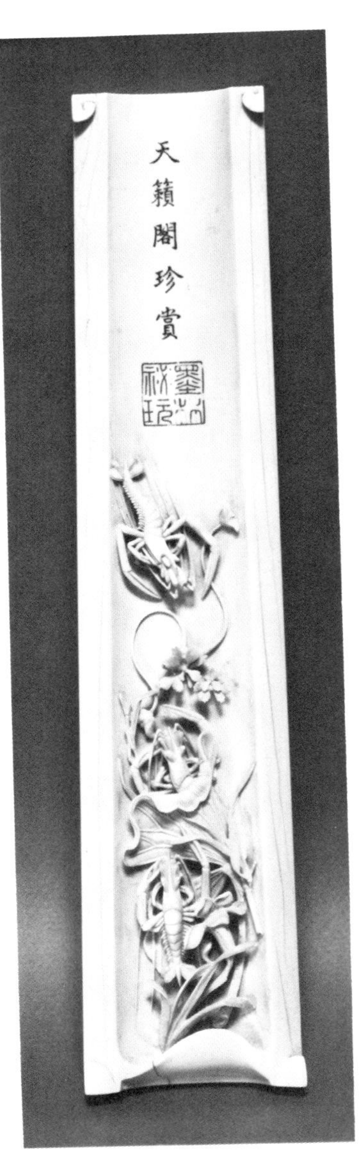

Fig. 47. *Brush with Carved Designs*. Bamboo, animal hair, inscribed "Made in the Reign of Wan-li of Great Ming," 1573–1619. Anonymous gift. CMA 67.194

wrist rest is decorated with shrimp surrounded by water plants carved in low relief. A disciplined calligrapher rested his arm against this artistic implement to ensure a steady hand while writing stylized scripts. Those calligraphers who worked without the benefit of a wrist rest simply supported their writing arm with the free hand.

In contrast to the airy, delicately carved details enlivening these small accessories, the simplicity and elegance of the Kuan ware brush washer (Fig. 49) and brush rest (Fig. 50) illustrate the aesthetic sophistication that distinguishes the arts of the earlier Sung Dynasty. Kuan ware, one of the classic ceramics of this era that was used only by the imperial court, was manufactured in the suburbs of the capital, Hangchou. Its thinly potted, dark body, covered with a thick glaze of pale gray, is still evident on the rim of the brush washer and the curving top of the brush rest. Like all other celadons, the color of the glaze is the result of small quantities of iron that produce a variety of tones ranging from a pale gray to blue green when fired in an oxygen-poor (reduction) kiln. Described in twelfth-century texts as a "crab-claw" pattern, the dark, crackled network accenting the glaze appeared for the first time during this period and was an intentional, desirable characteristic. These exclusive accessories of the scholar's table reflect the courtly taste of the twelfth century. The profile of the brush

Fig. 48. *Wrist Rest*. Ivory. Ming Dynasty, 1368–1644. Purchase, Edward L. Whittemore Fund. CMA 77.9

Fig. 49. *Square Brush Washer*. Kuan stoneware. Southern Sung-Yüan dynasties, 12th–14th centuries. Purchase from the John L. Severance Fund. CMA 57.41

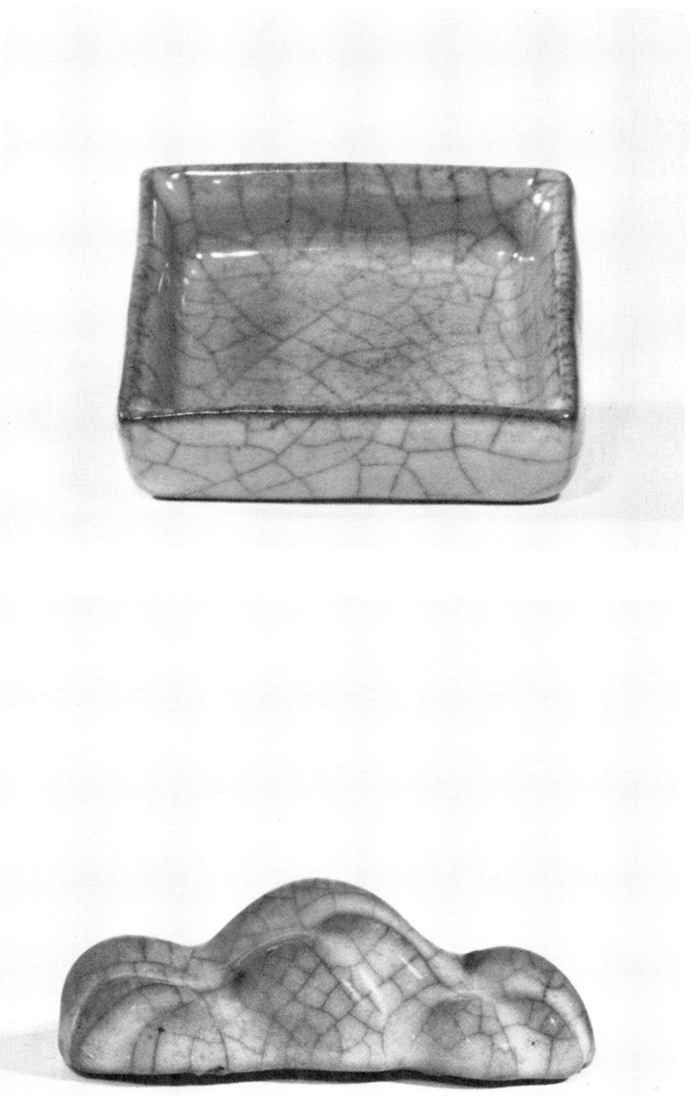

rest suggests the mountain retreats of Taoist immortals, a fitting symbol for a scholarly, artistic abode.

Close friends visiting a scholar's studio would find within the room objects that did not function as artistic materials nor as a part of his library or collection of antiquities. Included among these so-called eccentric objects were nature's unusual creations, such as oddly shaped rocks eroded by water or wind and gnarled pieces of wood (Fig. 51) whose very presence conveyed age and endurance. Scholars, particularly during the Ming and Ch'ing dynasties, enthusiastically collected these often bizarre articles to furnish their studios and embrace nature's forms in their own private worlds.

A cultlike passion for rocks[15] and mountains has persisted among the Chinese since antiquity. Emperors, scholars, and merchants all scavenged the distant provinces, retrieving rocks with peculiar geological formations to enhance their private gardens. Fancifully shaped rocks, such as the tall vertical stone standing near Wu Chen's pavilion in his handscroll *Poetic Feeling in a Thatched Pavilion* (Fig. 36), have been mistaken by Western viewers for imaginary creations; in reality, like Chü-jan's "alum-head" stones (see Figs. 19, 20) they are derived from prototypes in the physical world. Other rocks selected for the artist's studio might be "picture-rocks" whose natural colorings and formations imply

Fig. 50. *Brush Rest*. Kuan stoneware. Southern Sung-Yüan dynasties, 12th–14th centuries. Purchase from the John L. Severance Fund. CMA 57.42

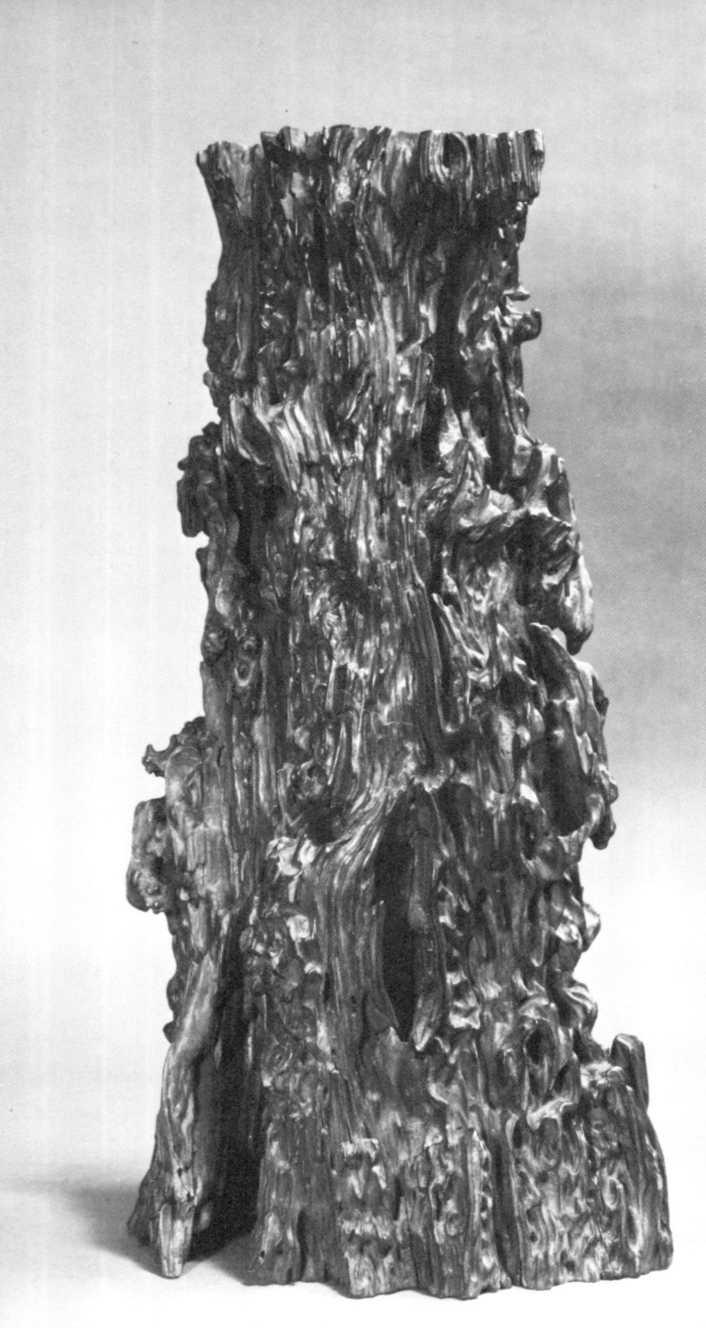

fantastic animals or the mountains and mist of Sung Dynasty landscape paintings. Still others represent miniature mountains, the dwellings of such Confucian hermits as Hsü Yu (see Fig. 25), Buddhist deities, and Taoist immortals. These miniature mountains, when grouped together, could symbolize the five cosmic mountains (T'ai shan, Hua shan, Heng shan, Huo shan, and Sung shan).

Unlike the painted "type-forms," such as Li Ch'eng's "crab-claw" tree (see Figs. 15, 16), eccentric objects were selected because of peculiar appearances that distinguished them from nature's more common forms. A Ch'ing Dynasty connoisseur chose a prunus stump (Fig. 51), partially carved to accentuate its naturally textured surface, for its exceptional form. Fascination for trees with gnarled forms and textured surfaces was shared by artists throughout the entire history of Chinese painting. Ching Hao, a tenth-century artist and critic, sketched one such pine until it "became real" to him while the eighteenth-century painter Li Shan dramatically depicted in a hanging scroll, *Five Pine Trees* (see Fig. 34), intertwining, bark-covered trunks and branches. A love for the seemingly artificial, bizarre, or unnatural shapes is characterized by such natural creations as this wizened prunus wood.

As segregated elements of the natural world, these eccentric objects symbolize the literati, whose scholarship and integrity set them apart from the rest of humanity. As accessories in the artist's studio they shared an exclusive realm where the woods were deep, the bamboos and pines clean, and the dust distant.

Fig. 51. *Prunus Wood*. Ch'ing Dynasty, 1644–1911. Anonymous loan.

Notes

1. William Theodore de Bary, ed., *Sources of Chinese Tradition* (New York: Columbia University Press, 1960), p. 25.

2. Laurence Sickman and Alexander Soper, *The Art and Architecture of China* (Baltimore, Maryland: Penguin Books, 1917), p. 133.

3. Thomas Lawton, *Chinese Figure Painting* (Washington, D.C.: Smithsonian Institution, 1973), p. 9.

4. Sherman E. Lee, *Chinese Landscape Painting* (Cleveland, Ohio: Cleveland Museum of Art, 1954), p. 8.

5. Richard Edwards, ed., *The Painting of Tao-chi*, exh. cat., Museum of Art, University of Michigan (New Haven, Connecticut: Eastern Press, 1967), p. 23.

6. Lee, *Chinese Landscape Painting.* p. 8.

7. James Cahill, *Hills Beyond a River: Chinese Painting of the Yüan Dynasty, 1279–1368* (New York: Weatherhill, 1976), p. 87.

8. Kuo Hsi, *An Essay on Landscape Painting: Lin Ch'üan Kao Chih*, trans. Shio Sakanishi (New York: Grove Press, 1935), p. 33.

9. Sickman and Soper, *The Art and Architecture,* p. 486.

10. Susan Bush, *The Chinese Literati on Painting: Su Shih (1037–1101) to Tung Ch'i-ch'ang (1555–1636)* (Cambridge, Massachusetts: Harvard University Press, 1971), p. 31.

11. Cahill, *Hills Beyond a River*, p. 70.

12. Kuo Hsi, *An Essay on Landscape Painting*, (New York: Grove Press, 1935), p. 37.

13. The fourteenth-century text *The Essential Criteria of Antiquities* [*Ko Ku Yao Lun*]. in the chapter entitled "Studio Objects," points out that windows covered with greased paper were brighter and advises the use of sesame oil in reading lamps: it burns without smoke so that it is "kind to the eyes." See Percival David, ed. and trans., *Chinese Connoisseurship* [*Ko Ku Yao Lun*]: *The Essential Criteria of Antiquities* (London: Faber and Faber, 1971), p. 211.

14. Wai-kam Ho, *Chinese Art Under the Mongols: The Yüan Dynasty, 1279–1368* (Cleveland, Ohio: Cleveland Museum of Art, 1968), p. 91.

15. For further information on stone collecting, see Edward H. Schafer, *Tu Wan's Stone Catalogue of Cloudy Forest: A Commentary and Synopsis* (Berkeley and Los Angeles: University of California Press, 1961).

Selected Bibliography

Cahill, James. *Chinese Painting*. Geneva: Albert Skira, 1960.
______. *Hills Beyond a River: Chinese Painting of the Yüan Dynasty, 1279–1368*. New York: Weatherhill, 1976.
______. *Parting at the Shore: Chinese Painting of the Early and Middle Ming Dynasty, 1360–1580*. New York: Weatherhill, 1978.
Chinese Art Under the Mongols: The Yüan Dynasty (1279–1368), exh. cat., with essays by Sherman E. Lee and Wai-kam Ho. Cleveland, Ohio: Cleveland Museum of Art, 1968.
de Bary, William Theodore, ed. *Sources of Chinese Tradition*. New York: Columbia University Press, 1960.
Eight Dynasties of Chinese Painting: The Collections of the Nelson Galley-Atkins Museum, Kansas City, and The Cleveland Museum of Art, exh. cat., with essays by Wai-kam Ho, Sherman E. Lee, Laurence Sickman, and Marc F. Wilson. Cleveland, Ohio: Cleveland Museum of Art, 1980.
Fei Ch'eng-wu. *Brush Drawing in the Chinese Manner*. London and New York: Studio Publications, 1956.
Gulik, R. H. van. *Chinese Pictorial Art as Viewed by the Connoisseur*. Roma: Instituto Italiano Per Il Medio Ed Estremo Oriente, 1958.
Lawton, Thomas. *Chinese Figure Painting*, exh. cat., Freer Gallery of Art Fiftieth Anniversary Exhibition. Washington, D.C.: Smithsonian Institution, 1973.
Lee, Sherman E. *Chinese Landscape Painting*, exh. cat. Cleveland, Ohio: Cleveland Museum of Art, 1954.
______. *The Colors of Ink: Chinese Paintings and Related Ceramics from The Cleveland Museum of Art*, exh. cat. New York: Asia Society, 1974.
March, Benjamin. *Some Technical Terms of Chinese Painting*. Baltimore, Maryland: Waverly Press, 1935.
Sickman, Laurence, and Soper, Alexander. *The Art and Architecture of China*. Baltimore, Maryland: Penguin Books, 1971.
Sullivan, Michael. *Symbols of Eternity: The Art of Landscape Painting in China*. Stanford, California: Stanford University Press, 1979.

Photographic Credits

Freer Gallery of Art, Washington, D.C.: Fig. 31

Nicholas C. Hlobeczy: Figs. 1, 3, 4, 5, 6, 7, 11, 12, 17, 18, 19, 21, 22, 23, 25, 26, 27, 28, 29, 30, 32, 33, 34, 35, 36, 37, 38, 39, 40, 41, 42, 43, 44, 45, 46, 47, 48, 49, 50, 51

Martin Linsey: Figs. 2, 8, 10, 16, 20, 24

Nelson Gallery-Atkins Museum, Kansas City: Figs. 9, 13, 14, 15

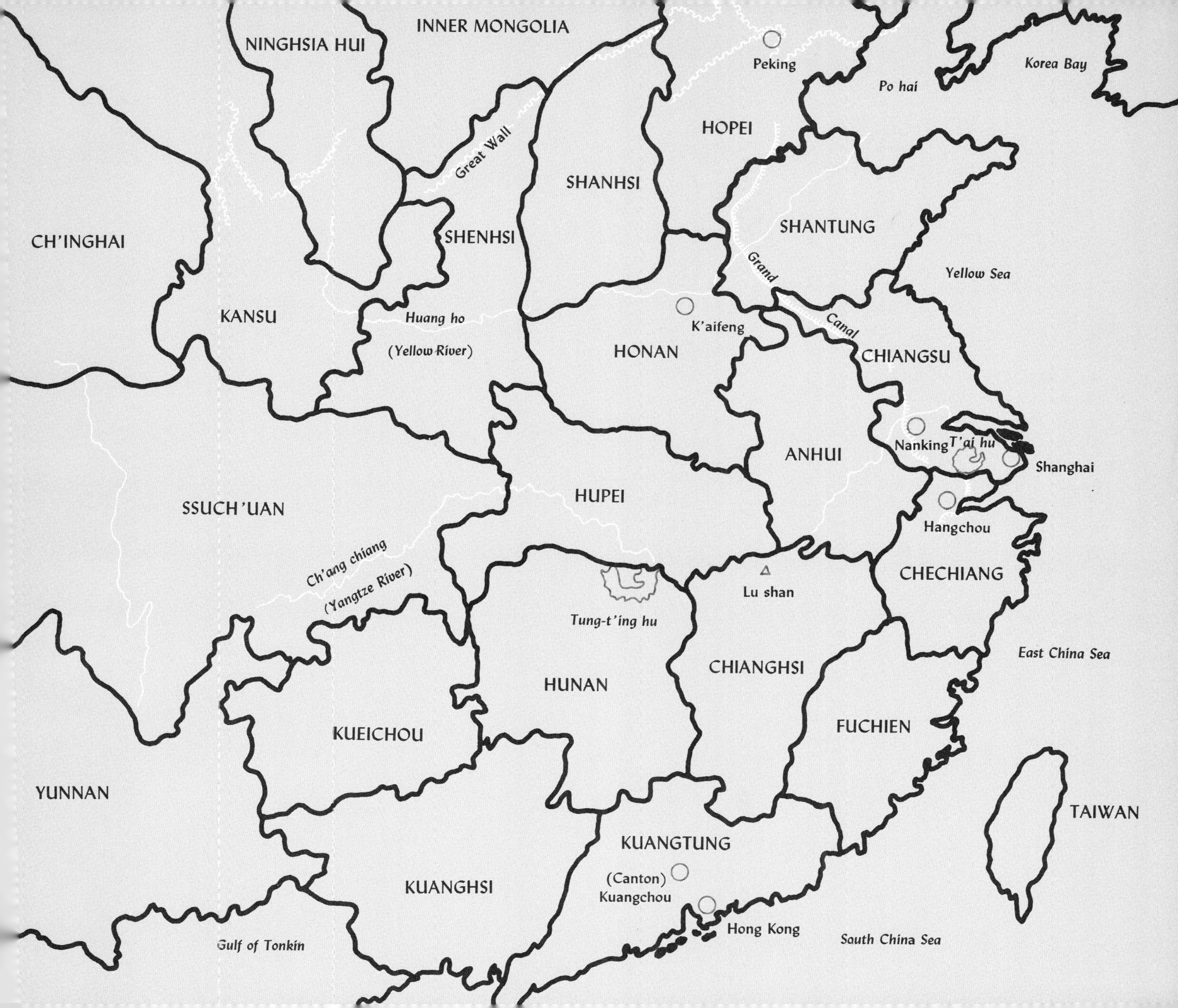

INNER MONGOLIA
NINGHSIA HUI
Peking
Po hai
Korea Bay
Great Wall
HOPEI
SHANHSI
SHANTUNG
CH'INGHAI
SHENHSI
Grand
Yellow Sea
KANSU
Huang ho
(Yellow River)
K'aifeng
HONAN
Canal
CHIANGSU
Nanking
T'ai hu
Shanghai
ANHUI
SSUCH'UAN
HUPEI
Hangchou
Ch'ang chiang
(Yangtze River)
Lu shan
CHECHIANG
Tung-t'ing hu
East China Sea
CHIANGHSI
HUNAN
KUEICHOU
FUCHIEN
YUNNAN
TAIWAN
KUANGTUNG
KUANGHSI
(Canton)
Kuangchou
Hong Kong
South China Sea
Gulf of Tonkin

Themes in Art Series

This volume is one of a series of paperback books about art, art history and artistic expression published by the Art History and Education Department of The Cleveland Museum of Art under the general editorship of Dr. Gabriel P. Weisberg, curator of art history and education. These books are available at The Cleveland Museum of Art or through Indiana University Press, Bloomington, IN 47405.

American Folk Art: From the Traditional to the Naive by Lynette I. Rhodes. 120 pp., 88 b&w illus., 6 color plates, 8½ x 7¼ inches, 1978. LC 77-9240, ISBN 0-910386-42-0.

American Realism and the Industrial Age by Marianne Doezema. 144 pp., 82 b&w illus., color cover, 4 color plates, 8½ x 7¼ inches, 1980. LC 80-67347, ISBN 0-910386-61-7.

The Artist and the Studio in the Eighteenth and Nineteenth Centuries by Ronnie L. Zakon. 68 pp., 40 b&w illus., color cover, 8½ x 7½ inches, 1978. LC 78-51885, ISBN 0-910386-40-4.

Between Past and Present: French, English and American Etching 1850-1950 by Gabriel P. Weisberg and Ronnie L. Zakon. 76 pp., 49 illus., 8½ x 7¼ inches, 1977. LC 76-53113, ISBN 0-910386-33-1.

Chardin and the Still-Life Tradition in France by Gabriel P. Weisberg with William S. Talbot. 94 pp., 77 b&w illus., 4 color plates, 8½ x 7¼ inches, 1979. LC 79-63386, ISBN 0-913086-51-x.

The Drawings and Water Colors of Léon Bonvin by Gabriel P. Weisberg, with an essay by William R. Johnston. 64 pp., 43 b&w illus., 5 color plates, 8½ x 7¼ inches, 1980. LC 80-20902, ISBN 0-910386-62-5.

Idea to Image: Preparatory Studies from the Renaissance to Impressionism by Mark M. Johnson, 84 pp., 96 b&w illus., 8½ × 7¼ inches, 1980. LC 79-93194, ISBN 0-910386-58-7.

In the Nature of Materials: Japanese Decorative Arts by Marjorie Williams, 48 pp. 8¾ x 11 inches, 33 b&w illus., 1977. LC 76-51970, ISBN 0-910386-32-3.

Materials and Techniques of 20th-Century Artists by Dee Driscole and Dorothy Ross, under the guidance of Gabriel P. Weisberg, Andrew T. Chakalis, Karen Smith, and June Hargrove. 48 pp., 31 b&w illus., 7½ x 9 inches, 1976. LC 76-29167, ISBN 0-910386-37-4.

The Public Monument and Its Audience by Marianne Doezema and June Hargrove. 72 pp., 62 b&w illus., 8½ x 7¼ inches, 1977. LC 77-25428, ISBN 0-910386-38-2.

Science within Art by Lynette I. Rhodes. 72 pp., 48 b&w illus., color cover, 8½ × 7 inches, 1980. LC 79-93193, ISBN 0-910386-57-9.

A Study in Regional Taste: The May Show 1919-1975 by Jay Hoffman, Dee Driscole, and Mary Clare Zahler, 72 pp., 70 b&w illus., 8½ x 7¼ inches, 1977. LC 77-78145, ISBN 0-910386-36-6.

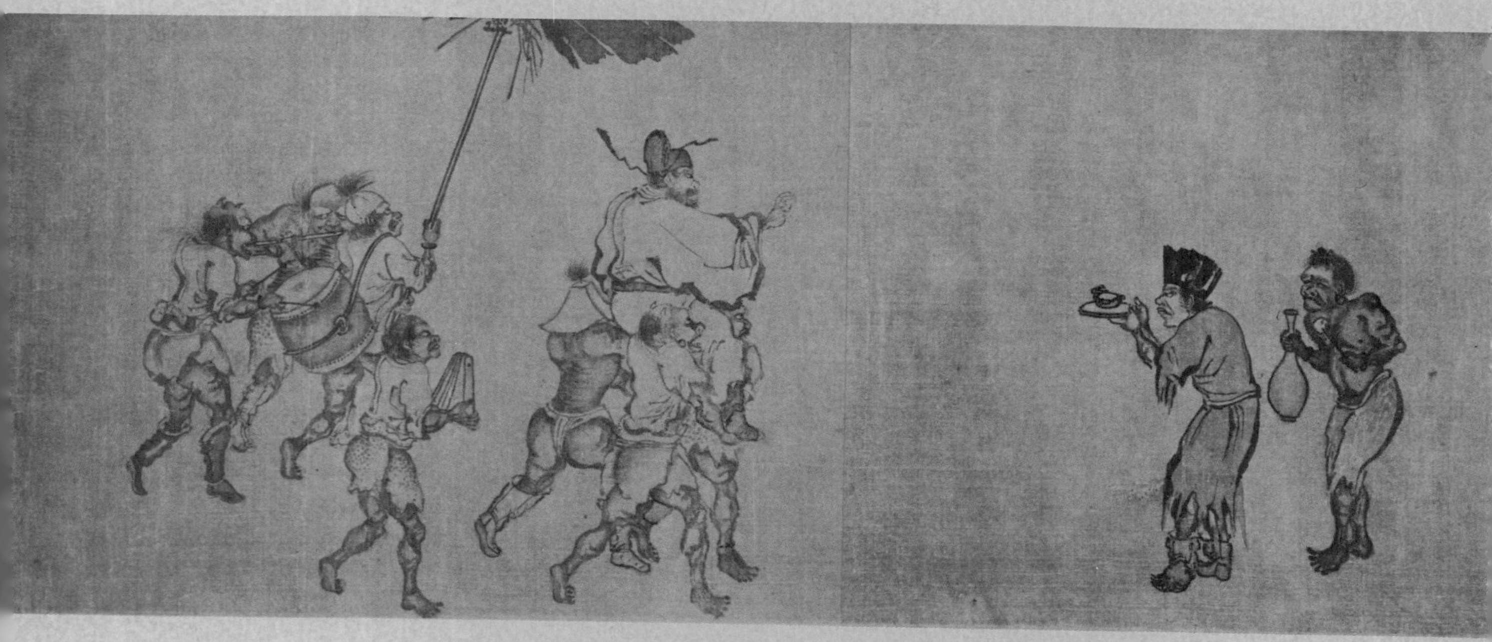

Fig. 4. *The Lantern Night Excursion of Chung K'uei.* Handscroll, ink on silk. Yen Hui, Yüan Dynasty, 14th century. Purchase, Mr. and Mrs. William H. Marlatt Fund. CMA 61.206 [91]

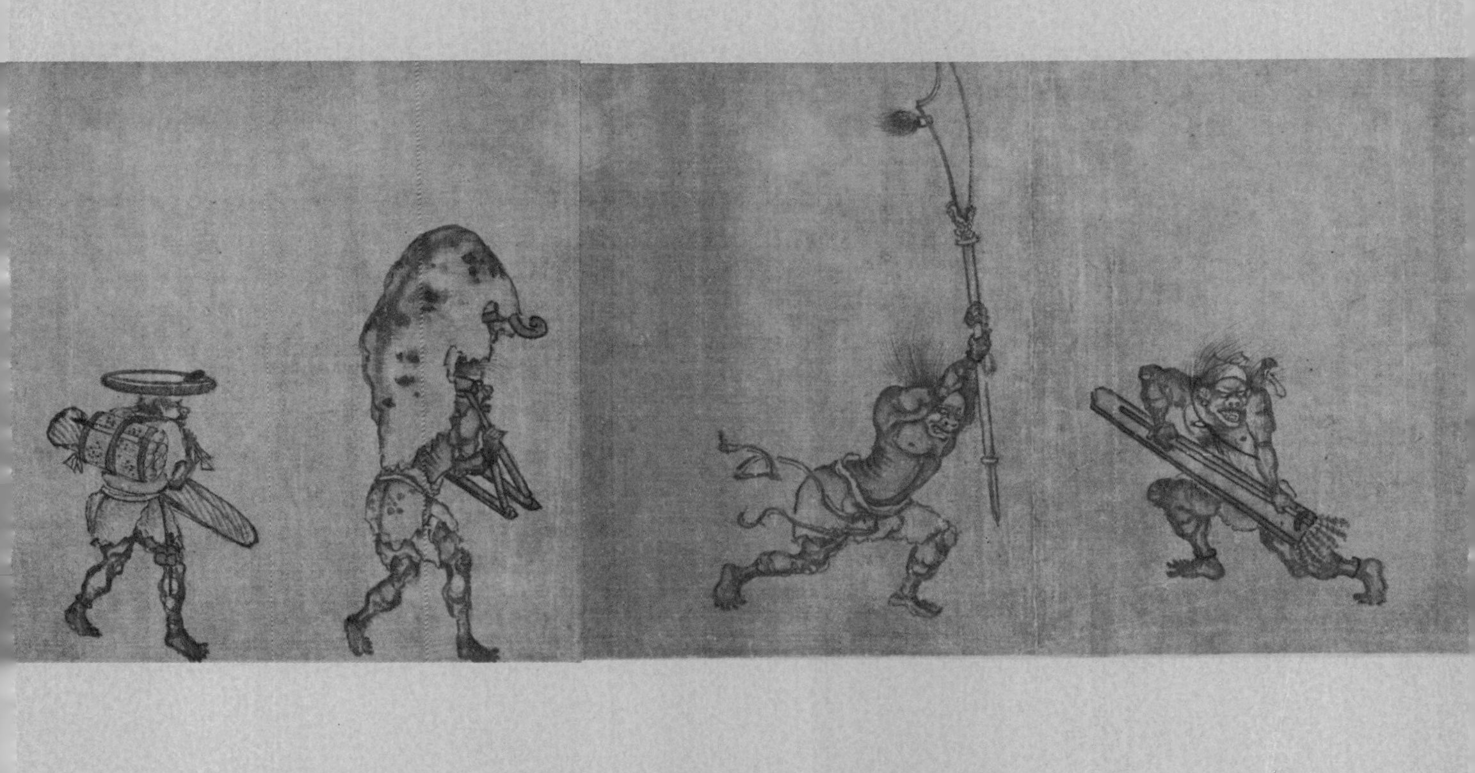

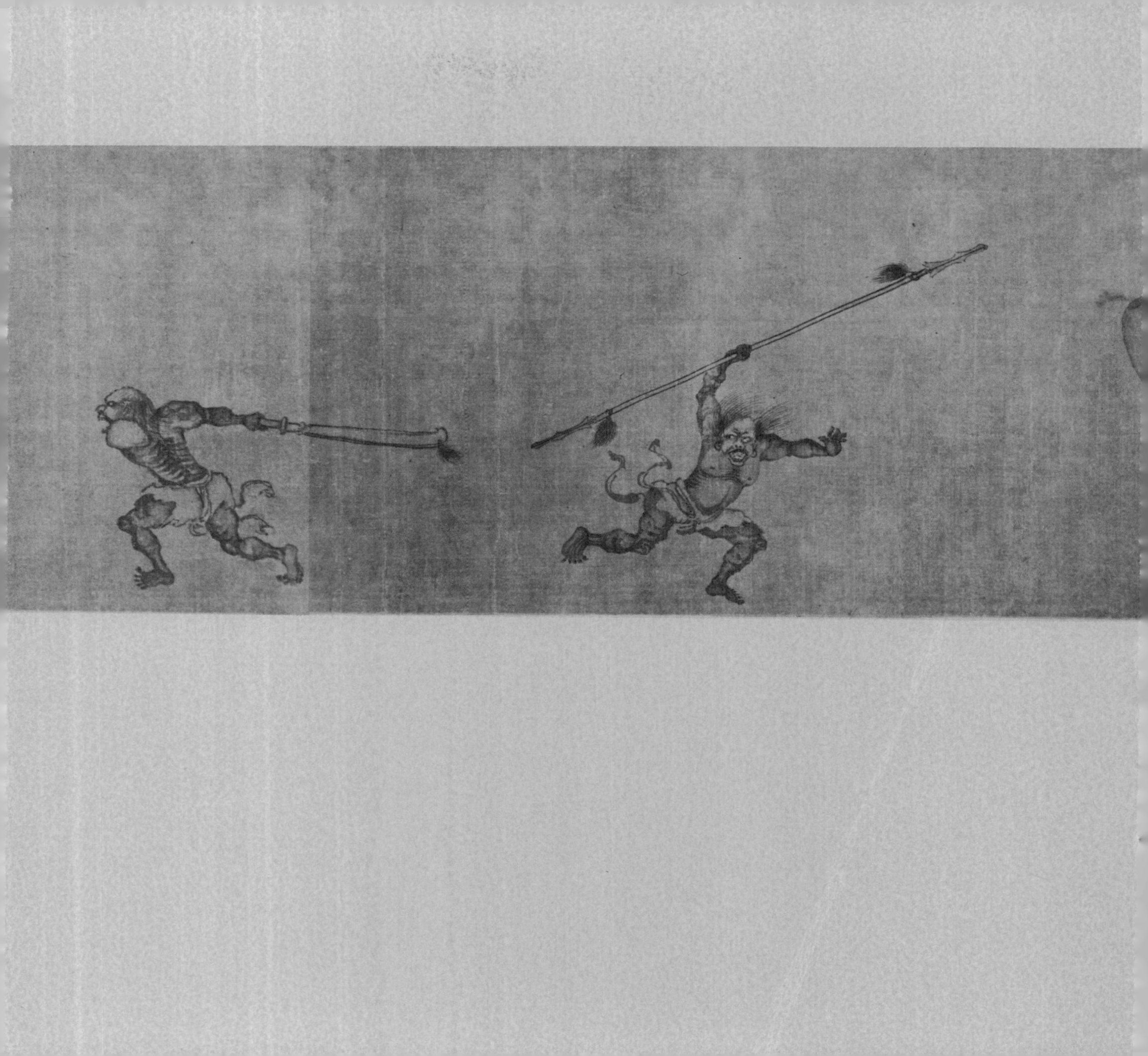

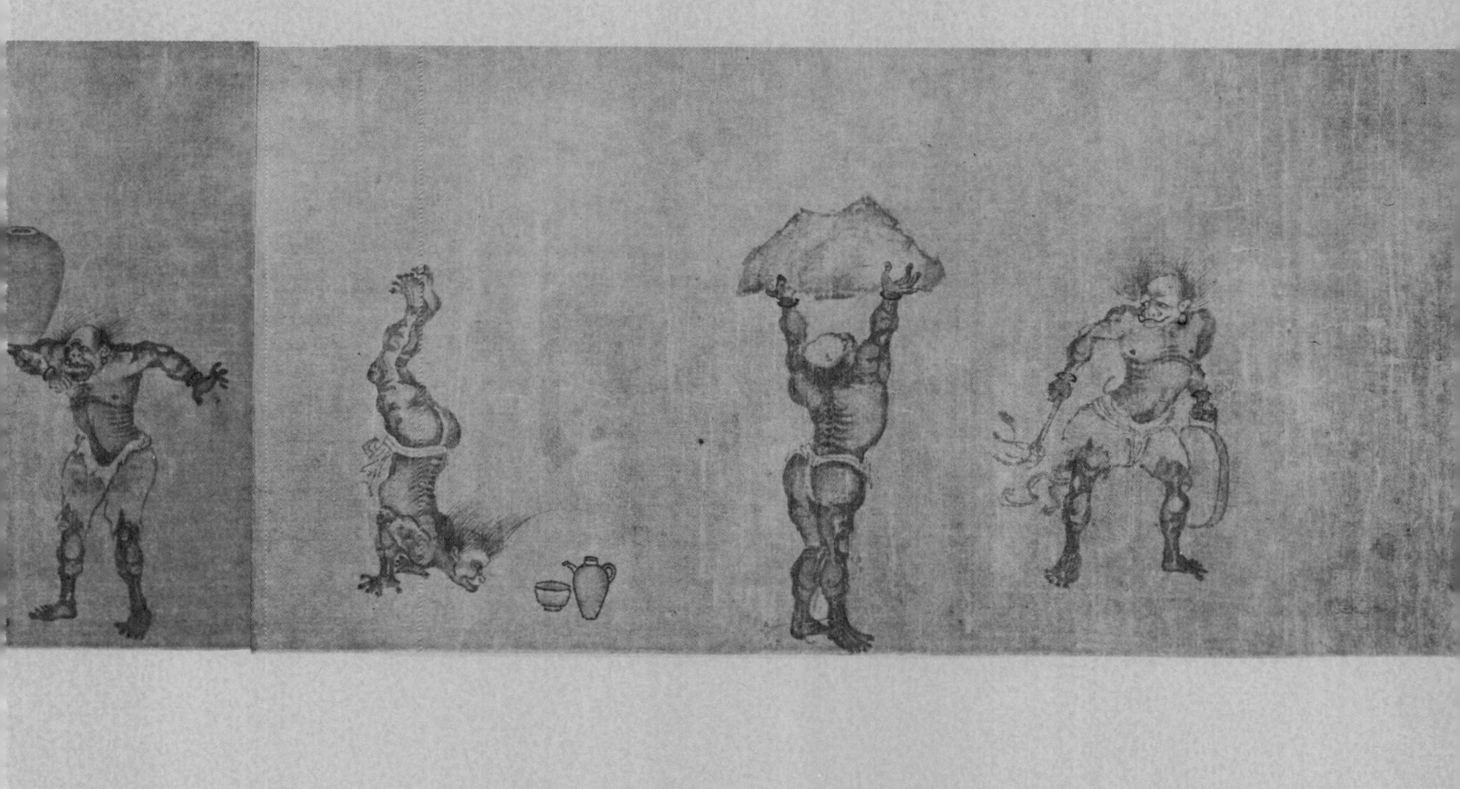